DATE		
Room	205 or 209	2-15-07

SCIENCE PROJECT IDEAS

Science Project Ideas About

SPACE SCIENCE

Revised Edition

Robert Gardner

Enslow Publishers, Inc.

40 Industrial Road   PO Box 38
Box 398   Aldershot
Berkeley Heights, NJ 07922   Hants GU12 6BP
USA   UK

http://www.enslow.com

Library of Congress Cataloging-in-Publication Data

Gardner, Robert, 1929–
  Science project ideas about space science / Robert Gardner.—Rev. ed.
     p. cm. — (Science project ideas)
  Originally published as: Projects in space science
  Includes bibliographical references and index.
  ISBN 0-7660-1707-9
  1. Space sciences—Experiments—Juvenile literature. [1. Space
sciences—Experiments. 2. Experiments. 3. Science projects.] I. Title.
QB500.264 .G375   2002
520'.78—dc21

                                             2001000705
Printed in the United States of America

10 9 8 7 6 5 4 3 2 1

This book was originally published in 1988 by Julian Messner as *Projects in
Space Science*.

To Our Readers: We have done our best to make sure all Internet addresses in
this book were active and appropriate when we went to press. However, the
author and the publisher have no control over and assume no liability for the
material available on those Internet sites or on other Web sites they may link to.
Any comments or suggestions can be sent by e-mail to comments@enslow.com or
to the address on the back cover.

Illustration Credits: Stephen F. Delisle, pp. 13, 81; Enslow Publishers,
Inc., p. 76; Gary Koellhoffer, Crooked Grin Design, pp. 11, 12, 15, 17, 20,
21, 23, 41, 43, 44, 48, 60, 67, 74, 84, 89, 92, 101, 114, 121; Jacob Katari,
p. 18 ; Stephanie Rowland, pp. 72, 73.

Cover Photo: Jerry McCrea (foreground); NASA/STScI/AURA
(background)

CONTENTS

INTRODUCTION

In this book you will find experiments about space. The experiments use simple everyday materials you can find at home or at school.

The book will help you to work the way real scientists do. You will be answering questions by doing experiments to understand basic scientific principles.

Most of the experiments provide a lot of guidance. But some of them will raise questions and ask you to make up your own experiments to answer them. This is the kind of experiment that could be a particularly good start for a science fair project. Such experiments are marked with an asterisk (*).

Please note: **If an experiment uses anything that has a potential for danger, you will be asked to work with an adult.** *Please do so! The purpose of this teamwork is to prevent you from getting hurt.*

Science Project Ideas About Space Science can open science's door to you—and draw you out into the mysterious world of space!

MEASUREMENT ABBREVIATIONS			
astronomical unit	AU	**kilometers**	
centimeter	cm	**per second**	km/s
Celsius	C	**light-year**	ly
Fahrenheit	F	**meter**	m
foot	ft	**meters per second**	m/s
feet per second	ft/s	**mile**	mi
inch	in	**miles per hour**	mph
kilometer	km	**miles per second**	mi/s
kilometers		**milliliter**	mL
per hour	km/hr	**second**	s

SAFETY FIRST

As you do the activities and experiments described in this or any other book, do them safely. Keep in mind the rules listed below and follow them faithfully.

1. Any experiments that you do should be done under the supervision of a parent, teacher, or another knowledgeable adult.

2. Read all instructions carefully. If you have questions, check with an adult. Do not take chances.

3. If you work with a friend who enjoys science too, maintain a serious attitude while experimenting. Horseplay can be dangerous to you and to others.

4. Do not taste chemicals unless instructed to do so. Many of them are poisonous.

5. Keep flammable materials such as rubbing alcohol away from flames and other sources of heat.

6. If you are using matches or flames, have a fire extinguisher nearby and know how to use it.

7. Keep the area where you are experimenting clean and organized. When you have finished, clean up and put away the materials you were using.

8. Do not touch glass that has just been heated. If you should get burned, rinse the area with cool water and notify an adult.

9. Never experiment with the electricity that comes from wall outlets unless under the close supervision of a knowledgeable adult.

10. Never look directly at the Sun, it can cause permanent damage to your eyes.

You can add to the value of the experiments you do by keeping notes on them. Set up an experiment notebook and record carefully the work you do and details like amounts and time involved. In doing some of these experiments, you may discover new questions that you can answer with experiments of your own. By all means, carry out these experiments (with your parents' or teacher's permission). You are developing the kind of curiosity that is shared by all scientists.

THE NEARBY SKY

If you step outside on a clear day and look upward, you will see a blue dome we call the sky. **Never look directly at the Sun, it can cause permanent damage to your eyes.** The Sun, sometimes the Moon, and, if you look very carefully, the planet Venus can be seen on the surface of this dome, known to astronomers as the celestial hemisphere. At night you can see thousands of stars, sometimes the Moon, and often one or more planets. To most people, stars seem to be scattered across the sky in a random way. But others see definite patterns in the stars.

The Sun, which is the brightest star we see, rises and sets every day giving us day and night. There are two explanations for the Sun's motion. One is that the Sun makes a circular path about Earth each day. The other is that Earth turns about its axis each day, which makes the Sun appear to move around Earth. You are probably convinced that the second explanation is the correct one, but do you have good experimental evidence to support your belief?

Where Are We?

Positions on Earth are established from a giant imaginary grid that covers Earth's surface. These are the lines you see on maps or a globe. The lines that run north-south are called *meridians*. These lines measure *longitude*. The prime meridian is zero degrees longitude. It runs from the North Pole to the South Pole through Greenwich, England. If you look on a globe, you will see that the distance between these longitude lines is greatest at the equator. The lines join to form a point at each pole.

The Sun seems to move in a circle about Earth once every 24 hours. Since there are 360 degrees in a circle, the Sun moves 15 degrees of longitude every hour. That is why time zones are about 15 degrees apart. When you move westward from one time zone to the next, you set your clock back one hour. Why aren't all time zones exactly 15 degrees apart?

Imaginary lines parallel to the equator are called *parallels*. They are used to measure latitude—degrees north or south of the equator. Degrees of latitude are about 111 km (69 mi) apart. The North Pole is 90 degrees latitude. The equator is 0 degrees latitude. This book was written at 42 degrees latitude.

Experiment 1.1

YOUR LATITUDE

To do this experiment you will need:

✔ straw	✔ washer, nut, or sinker
✔ square piece of cardboard	✔ string
✔ protractor	✔ paper clip
✔ tape	✔ a friend

Do you know the latitude where you live? You can make a pretty good estimate of your latitude by measuring the altitude of the North Star (Polaris), which is located almost directly above Earth's North Pole. As you can see from Figure 1, the altitude—the angle of elevation above the horizon—of Polaris is equal to the latitude from which its altitude is measured. Because Polaris is so far from Earth, light rays coming from the star are nearly parallel. Any that were not parallel would not strike Earth.

To find Polaris, go outside on a clear night. Look to the northern half of the sky to find the Big Dipper. It consists of a group of bright stars that look like the side of a cooking pan or water dipper as you see in Figure 2. Depending on the season and the time of night, the Big Dipper

FIGURE 1

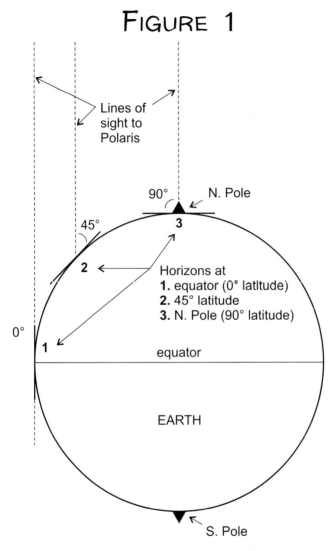

Lines of sight to Polaris

90°   N. Pole

3

45°

2

Horizons at
1. equator (0° latltude)
2. 45° latitude
3. N. Pole (90° latitude)

0°

1

equator

EARTH

S. Pole

may be turned at different angles in the sky. (See page 45 in Chapter 2.) The pointer stars, Dubhe and Merak, form a line that points toward Polaris. The distance of Polaris from the Big Dipper is about five times the distance between these two pointer stars. Do not expect to find a very bright star. Polaris is about as bright as Merak. It is the star at the end of the handle of the Little Dipper.

To measure the altitude of Polaris, you can build an astrolabe like the one shown in Figure 3. When you look at the North Star through the soda straw, the string will hang along a line that measures the star's altitude. What is the altitude of Polaris? What is the latitude of your location?

While you are measuring the North Star's altitude, have someone help you mark a north-south line of sight along level ground. While you

FIGURE 2

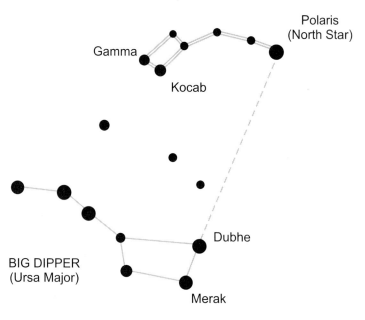

LITTLE DIPPER
(Ursa Minor)

Polaris
(North Star)

Gamma

Kocab

Dubhe

BIG DIPPER
(Ursa Major)

Merak

FIGURE 3

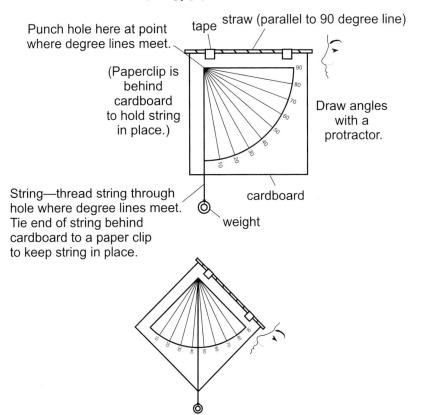

Punch hole here at point where degree lines meet.

tape straw (parallel to 90 degree line)

(Paperclip is behind cardboard to hold string in place.)

Draw angles with a protractor.

String—thread string through hole where degree lines meet. Tie end of string behind cardboard to a paper clip to keep string in place.

cardboard

weight

An astrolabe is turned upward; the string marks the altitude in degrees. If the star sighted is overhead, the string will lie on the 90 degree line.

stand looking at Polaris, you can direct your helper so that he or she is in line with Polaris. This will allow you to establish a straight line from the star to you. Markers at your position and the position of your helper will provide a north-south line that you will find useful in later experiments.

Experiment 1.2

THE SHIFTING SUN

To do this experiment you will need:

- ✔ an ADULT
- ✔ hand drill
- ✔ square board, about 30 cm (12 in) on a side
- ✔ ruler
- ✔ new, unsharpened pencil
- ✔ pencil sharpener
- ✔ sandpaper
- ✔ carpenter's level
- ✔ white paper
- ✔ scissors
- ✔ tape
- ✔ protractor
- ✔ tape measure
- ✔ map pins and mesh strainer, or colored pens and clear dome

The Sun does not follow the same path across the sky each day. The summer Sun follows a longer and higher path than does the winter Sun. To find the path of the Sun at various times of the year, you can build a sundial.

Ask an adult to drill a hole in a 30-cm (12-in) square board that has the same diameter as a new, unsharpened pencil. The hole should be near the center of one side of the board and about 5 to 7 cm (2 to 3 in) in from the side as shown in Figure 4. Break off the eraser end of the pencil and sharpen it. Then, to prevent

FIGURE 4

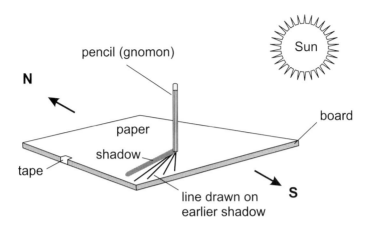

injury, break off the lead and sandpaper the end into a smoothly rounded surface. Insert the unsharpened end of the pencil into the hole in the board. The pencil should rise about 10 to 13 cm (4 to 5 in) above the surface of the board. Place the sundial on a level place along a north-south line such as the one you established while measuring the altitude of Polaris. The pencil, which is called the *gnomon*, should be near the south end of the board. Use a small carpenter's level to be certain the board is level and the pencil perpendicular to its surface.

Cover the board with a sheet of white paper. Cut a slit along the south edge of the paper so it will fit around the pencil, and tape the paper to the board.

Early in the morning, when the Sun begins to cast shadows of the pencil on the paper, you can begin making measurements. With a ruler, draw a line along the center of the shadow from the pencil to the end of the shadow. (If the shadow should extend beyond the board, place another board beside your sundial and measure the total length of the shadow.) Measure the shadow from the center of the pencil to the end of the shadow. Write the length of the shadow and the time you made the measurement along the line you have drawn. Repeat this procedure at frequent intervals throughout the day.

To check up on the north-south line you made, take frequent measurements of the pencil's shadow around midday. The shortest shadow cast by the pencil will occur when the Sun is due south. At that time, the pencil's shadow will lie along a north-south line. Is the pencil's shortest shadow parallel to the north-south line you established earlier?

After sunset you can bring the paper inside and determine the Sun's position in the sky at various times during the day. Draw a north-south line (through the shortest shadow) and east-west lines on your paper. Each line should pass through the point where the pencil was located.

The Sun's azimuth is its angle along the horizon relative to north. North is 0°; east is 90°; south is 180°; and west is 270°. With a protractor, determine the Sun's azimuth for each line you drew.

The Sun's altitude is its angle above the horizon. If the Sun is on the horizon, its altitude is 0°. If it is directly overhead, its altitude is 90°. To determine the Sun's altitude at each of the times you measured it, draw a vertical line equal to the height of the pencil. At the base of this line, draw a line equal to the length of the pencil's longest shadow. (This line should make a right angle with the line representing the height of the pencil.) Mark the length of the shadow for each of the times you measured it on this line. A line connecting the shadow's length and the pencil's height will enable you to find the Sun's altitude for each of the times you

FIGURE 5

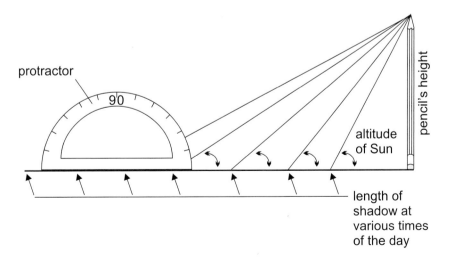

FIGURE 6

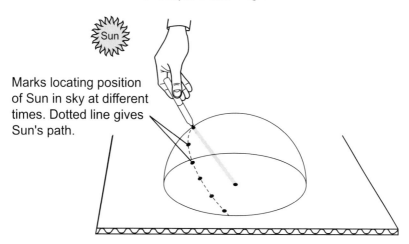

Marks locating position of Sun in sky at different times. Dotted line gives Sun's path.

marked the Sun's shadow. Just lay a protractor on the angle as shown in Figure 5.

With the information you have, you can map the Sun's position in the sky at each of the times you took a measurement with the sundial. (See Figure 6.) You could use map pins in a wire mesh strainer or colored pen marks on a clear dome. By saving this map of the Sun's path across the sky, you can compare it with other maps that you can make at different times of the year. To see the biggest changes in the Sun's path, make measurements at the beginning of each season—around the twentieth of March, June, September, and December.

When is the Sun's path across the sky longest? Shortest? Does the Sun always rise at an azimuth of 90 degrees and set at 270 degrees? When does the Sun reach its greatest altitude?

Experiment 1.3

A MODEL TO EXPLAIN SEASONAL CHANGES

To do this experiment you will need:

✔ light bulb	✔ cardboard tube
✔ table	✔ flashlight
✔ dark room	✔ white sheet of paper
✔ small globe or ball	✔ a partner
✔ tape	✔ pen or pencil

You know that the Sun's path across the sky changes from season to season. To explain seasonal changes on Earth, astronomers believe Earth's axis is tilted at 23.5° to its orbit about the Sun. To see how this affects sunlight falling on Earth, place a bright light bulb in the center of a table in a dark room. Then move a small globe or a ball in a large circle around the bulb. Keep the ball or globe tipped at the same angle (see Figure 7) as you move it along its circular path. Stop at point S and turn the ball or globe to represent Earth's rotation on its axis. In which part of Earth does the Sun never set when it is at point S? In which part does the Sun never rise?

FIGURE 7

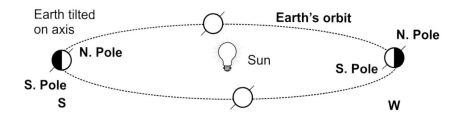

Repeat this process at point W. What seasons are represented by this model when Earth is at points S and W?

To see how the angle at which light strikes Earth affects a season's average temperature, tape a long section of a cardboard mailing tube to the end of a flashlight. Place the end of the cardboard tube several inches above, and perpendicular to, a white sheet of paper as shown in Figure 8. Have a partner mark an outline of the light that falls on the paper. Keeping the tube the same distance from the paper, tilt the flashlight and tube so that the light falls on the paper at a different angle. Again, have someone mark the outline of the light on the paper. Continue changing the angle that the tube makes with the paper until the tube is almost parallel with the paper.

FIGURE 8

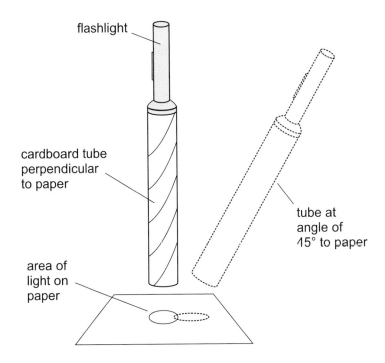

flashlight

cardboard tube
perpendicular
to paper

tube at
angle of
45° to paper

area of
light on
paper

The amount of light coming through the tube is constant, just as light emitted by the Sun is constant. But what happens to the area of the light on the paper as the tube moves from a position perpendicular to the paper to one that is nearly parallel? Which condition is closest to summertime? To wintertime? How is the area over which the light energy spreads related to the season's average temperature?

Experiment 1.4*

MOON CHANGES

To do this experiment you will need:

✔ pencil	✔ partner
✔ notebook	✔ tennis ball
✔ globe	✔ binoculars or telescope

Like the Sun, the Moon seems to circle Earth. But if you observe moonrise daily, you will see that it is about an hour later from one day to the next. You will notice, too, that the shape of the Moon changes dramatically over the course of a few days.

Try to observe the Moon over a period of several months. Make a daily sketch of its shape (when you can see it), a record of where it rises (azimuth) and/or sets, and its altitude and direction at different times. Do this as often as possible. You can make rough estimates of the azimuth and altitude using your fists. If you hold your fists at arm's length from your body, each fist occupies about 10 degrees. Try it! Hold your left fist so the top of your hand is level with the horizon. Then put your right fist on your left, then your left on your right, etc. You will find that it takes just about 9 fists to reach a point directly overhead (90° above the horizon).

How does the position of a rising full Moon compare with the position of the setting Sun on the same day? See if you can learn to predict the time, location, and shape of the rising Moon. How does the path of the Moon across the sky compare with the Sun's path?

You can make a model of the Moon's path about Earth that will help you understand why the Moon's shape changes. Place a globe, representing Earth, outside on a sunny day. Have a friend move a tennis ball about the globe, as shown in Figure 9, while you look at the ball with your eyes near the globe. Where, relative to Earth and the Sun, does the ball

FIGURE 9

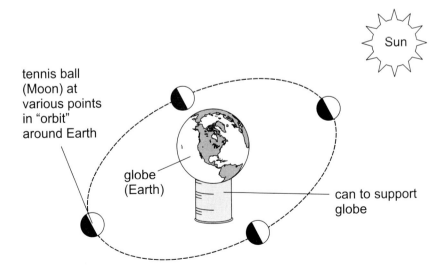

represent a full Moon as seen from Earth? A first quarter? A last quarter? A new Moon?

Using the model, when would you see a "full Earth" if you were on the Moon?

When Earth comes between the Moon and the Sun, Earth's shadow falls on the Moon, and we see an eclipse of the Moon. Where should the ball be placed to represent an eclipse of the Moon?

If the Moon comes between Earth and the Sun, it casts its shadow on Earth causing an eclipse of the Sun. Where should the ball be placed to represent an eclipse of the Sun? **Do not look at the Sun!**

Make a scale model of Earth and the Moon from the information given below about their diameters and separation. Attach "Earth" to one end of a long stick that represents the distance of Earth to the Moon on your scale. Attach the "Moon" to the other end. Take this model out into sunlight and move it about to produce eclipses. Why do eclipses occur so infrequently?

	Approximate distance
Earth to Moon	240,000 mi
Earth's diameter	8,000 mi
Moon's diameter	2,000 mi

Other Views of the Moon

To see the Moon when it is a crescent, just after a new Moon, you will have to view it shortly after sunset. You may be able to see a faint outline of the rest of the Moon as well as the bright crescent. This is sometimes called "the old Moon with the new Moon in its arms." The light beyond the crescent is due to earthshine— sunlight reflected from Earth to the Moon and then back to you.

If you have binoculars or a telescope, you will enjoy seeing a magnified image of the Moon and perhaps sense the same thrill that Galileo felt when he became the first human to view the lunar surface through a telescope. If you look along the terminator, the edge of darkness on the Moon, you will see that the long shadows cast there make the craters more distinct. Keep viewing the Moon from one new Moon to the next. You will notice that you always see the same side of the Moon. What does this tell you about the Moon's period of rotation (time to turn once on its axis) as compared with its period of revolution (time to make one complete orbit around Earth)?

Experiment 1.5*

A LOOK AT SOME PLANETS

To do this experiment you will need:

✔ clear dawn or dusk sky	✔ binoculars

After the Moon, the brightest object in the sky is Venus. It is often called the morning or evening "star." Of course, it is not a star. All the light we see from Venus, or any of the planets, is sunlight that is reflected from its surface. Because Venus is covered with clouds, 75 percent of the sunlight that strikes the planet is reflected. (Only 40 percent of the light striking Earth is reflected.) Since Venus's orbit is closer to the Sun than ours, Venus never appears very far from the Sun. Your newspaper will probably tell you the rising and setting times for Venus so that you should have no trouble finding it in the morning, before sunrise, or in the evening, after sunset, unless it happens to be very close to the Sun. Watch Venus for several months. What is the largest angle it makes with the Sun? You can use your fists to estimate this angle as the Sun sets or rises. **Remember: Never look directly at the Sun!**

If you locate Venus just before sunrise and keep track of its position, you will be able to see it even after the Sun rises. It is fun to point it out to others and show them that a "star" can be seen even in the daytime.

Again, with the newspaper to help you, you can probably locate the planet Jupiter, which is quite bright, and Mars, which is reddish. Mercury, which is never more than 28° from the Sun, and Saturn, the ringed planet, are more difficult to see, but with patience and perseverance you can find them. Binoculars will help, but if you are looking for Mercury **do not look while the Sun is in the sky.** There are a number of moons that orbit Jupiter, and you can see four of them with binoculars; however, you will probably have to mount the binoculars on a tripod or hold them against a firm object.

On a clear dark night you may see meteors, or shooting stars as they are often called. These are particles of matter that burn up when they hit Earth's atmosphere. There are particular places along Earth's orbit about the Sun where these particles seem to be concentrated. When Earth crosses these places, you have an opportunity to see forty or fifty meteors per hour "shower" through the sky. The Perseids shower can best be seen about August 12, and the Geminids shower about December 13. The showers are named for the constellation where they appear in the sky. Most newspapers will have an article about these two meteor showers just before they occur.

Bode's Law

During the late 1700s, astronomers developed a number scheme that became known as Bode's law. If you write down the series of numbers 0, 3, 6, 12, 24, 48, 96 . . . add 4 to each, and then divide each by 10, you obtain: 0.4, 0.7, 1.0, 1.6, 2.8, 5.2, 10.0. . . .

You may think these are just a bunch of random numbers, but the numbers were significant to astronomers who often measure distances in astronomical units (AU). One astronomical unit is the distance from Earth to the Sun 150,000,000 km (93,000,000 mi). If a planet were half as far from the Sun as Earth, the radius of its orbit would be 0.5 AU. A planet twice as far from the Sun as Earth would have an orbit with a radius of 2.0 AU.

Table 1 lists the planets and the radii of their orbits in astronomical units. Notice how closely the radii match the numbers in Bode's law. You can see why astronomers found Bode's law significant.

In 1781 the planet Uranus was discovered. It had a radius of 19.2 AU. This is close to the next number in the Bode's law series:

$$(192 + 4)/10 = 19.6.$$

TABLE 1.

SOME PLANETS AND THE RADII OF THEIR ORBIT IN ASTRONOMICAL UNITS (AU)

	Mercury	Venus	Earth	Mars	?	Jupiter	Saturn
Radius (AU)	0.38	0.72	1.0	1.52	2.8	5.2	9.54

The radii of the planets, including Uranus, are close to the numbers in the Bode's law series, but there is no planet at 2.8. During the nineteenth century, astronomers began to find small bodies at about 2.8 AU from the Sun, in the region between Mars and Jupiter. These bodies, with diameters of 1,000 km or less, are known as asteroids or minor planets. It used to be thought that the asteroids were the remnants of a planet that exploded. But it is more likely that they are particles from the original solar system that never came together to form a planet.

Meteors are believed to be material left by comets that broke up as they moved about the Sun. These particles continue to move along the comet's orbit—an orbit that crosses Earth's orbit.

Occasionally a comet will become visible as it moves close to the Sun. The orbits of comets are very long ellipses, unlike the nearly circular orbits of most planets.

A meteorite is a chunk of rock that has survived its fiery path through the atmosphere and struck Earth. Some meteorites have been huge. One that landed in Canada was nearly 3 km (2 mi) in diameter. An even larger one that struck Central America about 65 million years ago will be discussed in the next section. Fortunately, such large meteorites are very rare.

Life on Earth

Though nine planets (Mercury, Venus, Earth, Mars, Jupiter, Saturn, Uranus, Neptune, and Pluto) orbit the Sun, only Earth seems to harbor life. Mercury is sun-scorched, the surface of Venus, where it rains sulfuric acid, has a temperature of 480°C (870°F), and the planets from Jupiter outward are very cold. Astronauts found our barren Moon, which has no atmosphere or water, to be lifeless. There is evidence of water on Mars, but landings there in 1976 by *Viking 1* and *Viking 2* revealed no evidence of life. Future trips to the red planet may provide different results. On Earth, the evolution of plants that can produce oxygen and food from water and carbon dioxide has provided an oxygen-rich atmosphere where animal life can prosper.

In 1953, Harold Urey and Stanley Miller mixed water vapor, methane, and ammonia in a flask. These gases are thought to have been present in Earth's early atmosphere. Electric sparks, similar to the lightning flashes that were probably prevalent in Earth's early days, were sent through these gases. At the conclusion of the experiment, the flask contained a variety of organic substances including amino acids, the building blocks of proteins. We still do not know how these substances gave rise to life. But we do know that the basic chemical ingredients of life could have been produced in Earth's primitive atmosphere.

We know also that about 65 million years ago 65 percent of the existing species on Earth became extinct. Recently, scientists have found a thin layer of iridium-rich dust in sites that are about 65 million years old. Since iridium is an element commonly found in asteroids and meteoroids, some scientists believe that a giant meteorite may have slammed into Earth at that time spewing huge clouds of dust into the atmosphere. The dust so reduced the sunlight reaching Earth that temperatures fell below levels necessary for the survival of many plants and animals. Following this long winter, the dust gradually settled, allowing sunlight to fall in abundance again on a planet now devoid of many of its previous life-forms.

THE NEARBY SKY AND BEYOND

The nine planets and the asteroids that circle our Sun make up our solar system. But what is the origin of the solar system and the stars that we see beyond it?

It is believed that gravity pulls together the star dust from earlier stars that blew apart to form new planets and stars. Gravity is the force of attraction that one piece of matter exerts on another. This force depends on the amount of matter, commonly called mass, in each piece and the distance between the masses. If the mass of either piece is doubled, the pull between them (force of attraction) will double. If the distance between the pieces doubles, the force will be reduced to one fourth of its former value.

Earth pulls on you. The force it exerts on you is called your weight. If a larger person has twice your mass, the gravitational force between that person and Earth will be twice as great as the force between you and Earth. He or she will weigh twice as much as you do. But if you were to double your distance from the center of the Earth, the Earth's pull on you at this greater distance would be much less. Your weight would be quartered.

Originally, the rotating star dust that formed our solar system was very cold. The only gases that could exist at such low temperatures were hydrogen and helium. All other matter was probably in the form of solid dustlike particles. Gravitational pulls among the particles caused a general drift toward the center of the "cloud," producing a contraction of the matter and higher temperatures. Because of rotation, the cloud became a flattened disk. Near the center, where temperatures were higher due to greater pressure, a protosun formed. Rotation kept some of the matter far from the center—out where it was still very cold.

Continued contraction of the central part of the disk raised temperatures to millions of degrees. At such a high temperature, hydrogen began fusing to form helium, like a giant hydrogen bomb. The energy released by fusion kept that reaction going while creating an outward pressure that balanced the inward gravitational contraction. Thus a stable star, our Sun, was born.

The small, dense, inner planets, Mercury, Venus, Earth, and Mars, formed during a period of 100 million years as particles of matter circling the Sun, were pulled together by gravitational forces. These particles were rich in sulfur, silicon, iron, magnesium, and other metals from dead stars. The decay of radioactive elements, the violent impact of the colliding particles growing into planets, as well as heat from the growing star (Sun) nearby, kept these materials in a melted state. The denser iron sank beneath the lighter matter. This explains why Earth has an iron core surrounded by less dense rock and silicon-rich sand. The high temperature caused molecules of hydrogen and helium to move so fast that they escaped from the atmospheres of these inner planets.

For each planet there is an escape velocity. Anything moving faster than the escape velocity can escape the planet's gravity. On Earth, the escape velocity is 40,000 km/hr (25,000 mph).

Space probes sent from Earth to explore other planets had to be accelerated to the escape velocity in order to leave Earth and not be pulled back by gravity. The velocities of hydrogen and helium molecules, at the temperatures found on the inner planets, were large enough to escape the relatively weak gravity of these small planets.

The outer planets, Jupiter, Saturn, Uranus, and Neptune, are large and have low densities because so much of their matter is gaseous. They coalesced from particles of solid matter to form protoplanets. Temperatures so far from the Sun were low enough that the huge amounts of hydrogen and helium swept up by these planets as they moved along their orbits could not escape. As a result, the outer planets have Earth-sized cores of solid matter surrounded by thick gaseous atmospheres.

At about the time the planets reached their present size, the onset of fusion reactions at the Sun's core caused it to expel its outer matter. The solar system was essentially finished after the Sun began fusing hydrogen into helium.

The outermost planet, Pluto, does not have the characteristics of the other outer planets. Though it is so far away and so small that it is difficult to determine its properties very accurately, it appears to be more like an inner than an outer planet. One theory holds that

Pluto was once a moon of Neptune along with its present moons—Triton and Nereid, which have unusual orbits. An unknown planet passing close to Neptune, disturbed the orbits of Triton and Nereid. At the same time, it sent Pluto into a separate orbit about the Sun while tearing it into its present form, which includes its moon, Charon.

Table 2 contains information about each of the planets in our solar system.

TABLE 2.

ORBIT AND COMPOSITION DATA FOR THE NINE PLANETS

Planet	Radius of orbit (AU)	Time to orbit Sun (years)	Diameter (Earth = 1)	Mass (Earth = 1)	Density (g/cm³)
Mercury	0.39	0.24	0.38	0.06	5.4
Venus	0.72	0.62	0.95	0.82	5.2
Earth	1.0	1.0	1.0	1.0	5.5
Mars	1.52	1.88	0.53	0.11	3.9
Jupiter	5.2	11.86	11.3	318.0	1.3
Saturn	9.5	29.64	9.44	95.2	0.7
Uranus	19.2	84.01	4.10	14.5	1.2
Neptune	30.1	164.8	3.88	17.2	1.7
Pluto	39.4	247.7	0.2?	0.002?	1?

Experiment 2.1

A SCALE MODEL OF THE SOLAR SYSTEM

To do this experiment you will need:

✔ Table 2

You know from earlier experiments and reading that the diameter of the Sun is about 1,400,000 km (865,000 mi), the distance from Earth to Sun (the radius of Earth's orbit) is about 150,000,000 km (93,000,000 mi), and the diameter of the Earth is about 13,000 km (8,000 mi). Using this information and the data in Table 2, construct a scale model of the solar system. It will give you a good sense of the distances between planets.

The Milky Way

Stars are not spread evenly through space. They cluster in groups called galaxies. Our own Sun is but one of the billions of stars that make up our galaxy. On a clear, moonless night, away from city lights, you can see a hazy band that stretches across the sky. Look at this band with binoculars or a telescope. You will see that it is made up of a vast number of stars. These stars make up our galaxy. When we look at them, we are looking edge on into the Milky Way galaxy, the galaxy in which our own Sun lies.

The Milky Way galaxy is about 100,000 light-years (ly) in diameter. A light-year is the distance that light travels in one year. Since the speed of light is 300,000 km/s (186,000 mi/s), and since there are about 31 million seconds in a year, a light-year is a distance of about 6 trillion miles. So, our galaxy is 600,000 trillion miles across. Such distances are hard to imagine, especially when you realize that our solar system is *only* about 10 billion miles in diameter. This means that 60 million solar systems like ours could fit into our galaxy. When you realize that there are galaxies out to at least 12 billion light-years from us, you begin to appreciate the vastness of the universe we live in.

If an inch were used to represent the diameter of Earth, the solar system, on this scale, would stretch halfway to the Moon. The Milky Way galaxy would extend beyond the Sun to Saturn.

Galaxies are usually far apart, but telescopes reveal that they sometimes merge or collide. Since galaxies are only about 100 diameters (10 million ly) apart and stars within galaxies are about 100 million diameters apart, it is not surprising that galaxies collide more often than stars.

Constellations

The distance to the nearest star outside our solar system is about 4 light-years, but a near star may not appear as bright as a star that is much farther away. Stars that make up a constellation, such as the Big Dipper, may differ greatly in their distances from us. Between these bright stars are stars too dim to be seen with the naked eye. The stars that form a constellation are not necessarily very close together. And, because the stars in the constellations may be moving in different directions at different speeds, the constellations that we recognize today may look very different a few thousand years from now.

Because Earth moves about the Sun, the stars that we see when darkness falls change from month to month. The sky appears to turn about 30 degrees from one month to the next because Earth moves about 30 degrees along its 360-degree orbit in each of the 12 months. Ursa Major's position at 9 P.M. on October 1 will be the same as its position at 7 P.M. on November 1 or 11 P.M. on September 1. If you view the stars at the same time each night, they will appear to move about 2 hours (30 degrees) westward from one month to the next.

Experiment 2.2

A SKY CLOCK

To do this experiment you will need:

- ✔ 1/16-in-thick clear plastic (1 sq ft)
- ✔ scriber compass
- ✔ protractor
- ✔ marking pen
- ✔ plastic wrap
- ✔ heavy cardboard
- ✔ tape
- ✔ felt pen
- ✔ star chart
- ✔ flashlight
- ✔ red cellophane

Because the sky seems to rotate about Earth at a steady rate, you can build a sky clock that will allow you to tell time on clear nights. To make your sky clock you will need a 1-ft square sheet of 1/16-in-thick clear plastic. You can buy the plastic in an art store. Draw two straight lines forming right angles through the center of the sheet as shown in Figure 10. Place one point of a scriber attached to a compass at the center of the sheet. Use the other point of the scriber to scratch a circle with a radius of 5 1/4 in on the plastic sheet. Then draw additional circles with radii of 4 3/4, 4 1/4, and 3 in.

Use a protractor to break the circles into twelve 30 degree segments. With a marking pen,

FIGURE 10

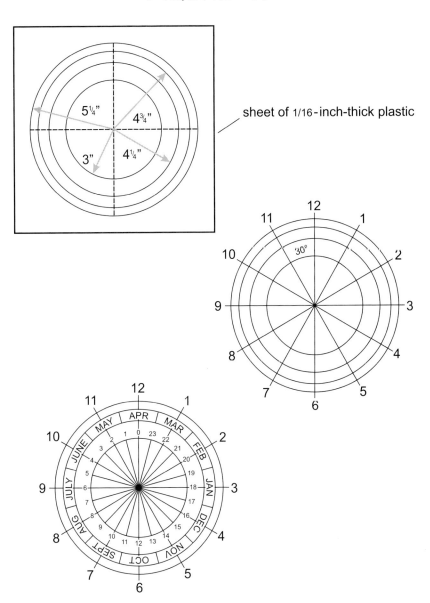

sheet of 1/16-inch-thick plastic

write the numbers found on a clock's face on your sky clock. Now divide each 30 degree segment in half. Use the marking pen to write in the months of the year, the 24 hours represented by the 15 degree lines, and to color the lines scratched in the plastic. The numbers representing hours on the 24-hour inner circle are numbered in counterclockwise fashion because Earth turns counterclockwise as viewed from Polaris.

Another, less expensive way to make a sky clock is to stretch a sheet of plastic wrap over a 1-ft-sq hole cut from a sheet of heavy cardboard. Tape the sheet firmly to the cardboard and draw the lines on the sheet with a felt pen.

Take your sky clock outside in the evening and early morning. Practice using it to tell time. Hold it so that its plane is perpendicular to, and its center in line with Polaris. The numeral 12 directly above April should be at the top of the clock as would be the numeral 12 on a clock in your house. Read the position of the pointer stars of the Big Dipper on your sky clock. Together they form a line representing the hour hand of a clock.

The drawings in Figure 11 show the 9 P.M. positions of the pointer stars at mid-month for each month of the year. Using those drawings, and the position of the pointer stars on your sky clock, you can make a good estimate of the time. For example, suppose it is mid-July. When you

FIGURE 11

JANUARY
(3 o'clock at 9 P.M.)

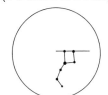

FEBRUARY
(2 o'clock at 9 P.M.)

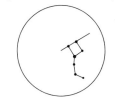

MARCH
(1 o'clock at 9 P.M.)

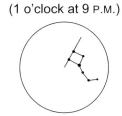

APRIL
(12 o'clock at 9 P.M.)

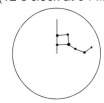

MAY
(11 o'clock at 9 P.M.)

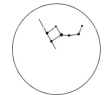

JUNE
(10 o'clock at 9 P.M.)

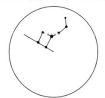

JULY
(9 o'clock at 9 P.M.)

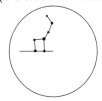

AUGUST
(8 o'clock at 9 P.M.)

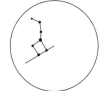

SEPTEMBER
(7 o'clock at 9 P.M.)

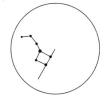

OCTOBER
(6 o'clock at 9 P.M.)

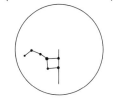

NOVEMBER
(5 o'clock at 9 P.M.)

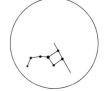

DECEMBER
(4 o'clock at 9 P.M.)

FIGURE 12

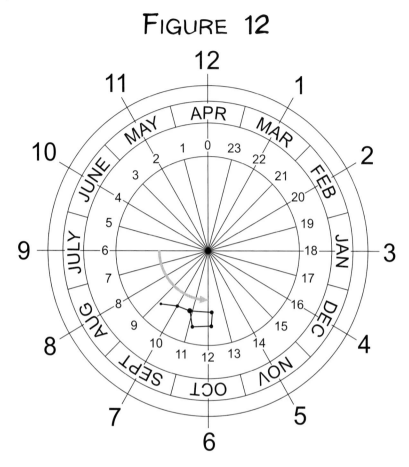

hold your sky clock properly, you see the pointer stars of the Big Dipper on your sky clock at the 6 o'clock position, as shown in Figure 12. The inner-numbered circle, which measures the 24 hours required for Earth to turn once on its axis, shows you that 6 hours (6 to 12) have passed since the pointer stars were at the 9 P.M. position, which is where they would be at 9 P.M. on July 15. Therefore, the time is 3 A.M.

Now, suppose it is November 23, and you see the pointer stars in the same 6 o'clock position. On November 15, at 9 P.M., you would expect the pointer stars to be in the 5 o'clock position. However, the inner circle shows you that these pointer stars are at a point 2 hours earlier than the 5 o'clock position (14 back to 12). If it were November 15, the time would be 7 P.M. Because it's about a week later than November 15, the clock position of the pointer stars at 9 P.M. will be at about 4:45. Consequently, the time is probably closer to 6:30 P.M.

With a little practice, you will be able to estimate time quite accurately with your sky clock. If you live near the eastern or western end of a time zone, your clock will appear to be a little fast or slow, and you will have to adjust your estimate accordingly. Since the sky clock is set for standard time, you will have to add an hour if you are on daylight saving time.

Polar Constellations

There are other bright constellations that turn about Polaris. A star chart will show you these constellations. The brighter the star, the bigger the dot on the chart.

Take a star chart outside. Bring a flashlight, but tape red cellophane over the glass in the flashlight. In that way, you will not loose your night vision when you shine the light on the chart. Place the appropriate month of the year uppermost against the northern sky to find the constellations. Can you find all the constellations on the chart?

Types of Stars

Stars are classified according to their surface temperature. Astronomers can determine a star's temperature by the type of light it emits. Red stars are cooler than blue stars as you can see from Table 3.

TABLE 3.
STAR TYPES AND THEIR CHARACTERISTIC TEMPERATURE AND COLOR

Star Type	Temperature (°C)	Color	Example
O	>35,000	greenish or bluish white	rare
B	10,000–35,000	hot white	Rigel in Orion
A	about 10,000	cool white	Sirius in Canis Major
F	6,000–10,000	slightly yellow	Polaris
G	about 6,000	yellow	the Sun
K	about 4,000	orange	Arcturus in Boötes
M	about 3,000	red	Betelgeuse in Orion

Experiment 2.3

A SPECTROSCOPE

To do this experiment you will need:

- ✔ scissors
- ✔ shoe box
- ✔ cardboard
- ✔ tape
- ✔ diffraction grating
- ✔ black construction paper
- ✔ showcase lamp or unfrosted light bulb
- ✔ fluorescent light bulb
- ✔ neon light
- ✔ large cardboard box
- ✔ white paper

To examine the light emitted by stars, astronomers use spectroscopes. A spectroscope is a device that separates light into the various colors that make it up. Light has wavelike properties, and we find that red light has a longer wavelength than blue light. To separate ordinary white light into its various colors or wavelengths, you can build a simple spectroscope.

Cut two small square holes in opposite ends of a shoe box. Cover one of the holes with two small pieces of cardboard so that they form a narrow slit as shown in Figure 13. Tape a piece of diffraction grating over the other hole. But before you fix it in place, hold it up toward a

FIGURE 13

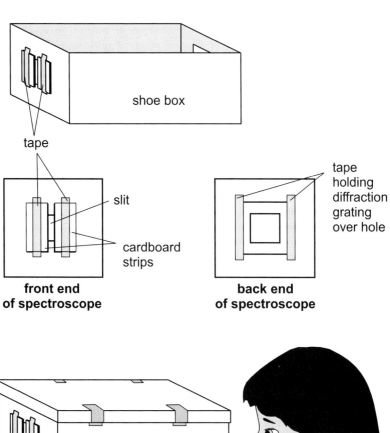

shoe box

tape

slit

cardboard
strips

tape
holding
diffraction
grating
over hole

**front end
of spectroscope**

**back end
of spectroscope**

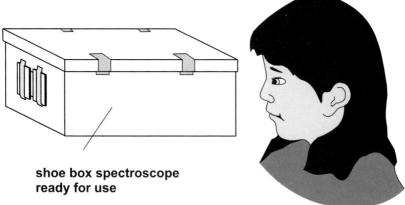

**shoe box spectroscope
ready for use**

light. Turn it so that when light comes through the grating the light spreads out into a *horizontal* spectrum of colors. You can buy diffraction gratings in a hobby shop or order one from a scientific supply company. Cover the rest of the inside of the box with black construction paper and tape it shut.

Hold the spectroscope so that the slit in the box is parallel with the bright filament of a showcase lamp or an unfrosted light bulb. Look to either side of the slit. You will see a spectrum containing all the colors of the rainbow. Look at a fluorescent light bulb. You will see not only a spectrum, but the bright violet, green, and yellow lines emitted by the mercury vapor inside the bulb. Like mercury, each element emits characteristic wavelengths or colors. Look at a neon light. What colors are released by neon? With spectroscopes, astronomers can figure out what elements are in stars.

To see the colors in sunlight, cut a small hole in one side of a large cardboard box. The hole should be in the middle of the side near the bottom. Tape a piece of diffraction grating over the hole. Then tape a sheet of white paper to the inside of the box on the side opposite the hole. Turn the box upside down and get inside with your back toward the diffraction grating. **Remember: Never look at the Sun.** Have a partner help you turn the box so that sunlight falls onto the grating. Look on the white screen to see the colors found in sunlight.

To view a solar eclipse, substitute a pinhole for the diffraction grating.

When a star is coming toward us at high speed, the wavelengths of the light it emits are shorter than normal. If the star is traveling away from us, its light waves are "stretched" into longer wavelengths. This phenomenon is known as the Doppler effect. You have probably observed this effect with sound. If a car is approaching you with its horn blaring, the pitch seems higher than normal because the vibrations are more frequent than normal. The sound waves are "squeezed" together because the horn is traveling toward you as it emits sound waves. Thus, one wave follows the next sooner than it would if the car were at rest. When the car passes you and moves away, the pitch seems lower than normal. The car is moving away from the waves that strike your ear, so the waves are "stretched" and reach you less frequently than they normally would.

In the case of receding stars, astronomers say the light has a red shift because the wavelengths of the light emitted are longer than would be the case if the star were at rest. Similarly, approaching stars show a blue shift. Knowing the speed of light and the amount that known wavelengths emitted by various elements in the stars are shifted, astronomers can determine the speed that stars are moving toward or away from us. By comparing the red shifts or blue shifts of stars turning on their axes, astronomers can tell which way a star is spinning. Further, from the red shifts seen in galaxies, there is good evidence that the universe is expanding and that the farther a galaxy is from us, the faster it is moving away.

3

MAN INTO SPACE

On October 4, 1957, the Soviet Union sent the world's first man-made satellite, *Sputnik 1*, into orbit. Most people were amazed to learn that *Sputnik* was moving about Earth at a speed of nearly 29,000 km/hr (18,000 mph). Yet, Sir Isaac Newton had shown how satellites could be launched from Earth almost 300 years earlier. All that was needed was the power to give the satellite the required speed.

After *Sputnik*, it was only a matter of time before man would journey into space. On April 12, 1961, the Soviet Union launched *Vostok 1*. On board was Yuri Gagarin, the first man to orbit Earth. Within the same decade, on July 20, 1969, as millions watched on television, American astronaut Neil Armstrong stepped onto the Moon and said, "That's one small step for man, one giant leap for mankind."

Today, people orbit Earth frequently, and some spend extended periods on the International Space Station. We talk of colonies in space where people may spend their entire lives, of mines on the Moon, and of future journeys to Mars. In this chapter we will look at the science that led to space travel.

Newton and Motion

Sir Isaac Newton was the first person to grasp the secrets of motion. And so it was he who first explained the pathway to space.

Through experimentation and careful creative thinking, Newton discovered three laws of motion. Before Newton, most people thought that an object moved only while a force (a push or a pull) acted on it. If the force was removed, the object would stop. Newton realized that a body stops, not because there is no force on it, but because a force opposes its motion. Usually this force is friction—the force between two surfaces when they rub together.

In his first law of motion, Newton stated that a body in motion will maintain its motion in the same direction unless acted upon by an outside force. A moving object continues to move in a straight line at a constant speed unless it's pushed or pulled by some force.

If you roll a marble along the floor, it continues to roll long after you stop pushing it. Of course, it will come to rest after awhile because there is some friction between the marble and the floor.

To see more dramatic evidence for Newton's first law of motion, you can build a frictionless car.

Experiment 3.1

FRICTIONLESS AIR CAR

To do this experiment you will need:

✔ an ADULT	✔ wooden spool
✔ ruler	✔ glue
✔ saw	✔ balloon
✔ 1/4-in-thick plywood or Masonite	✔ doll
✔ 1/16-in drill	✔ toy truck
✔ fine sandpaper	✔ bricks
	✔ strong rubber band

To build a small frictionless "car" you will need a balloon, a wooden spool (the kind thread comes on), a piece of 1/4-in-thick plywood or Masonite, glue, and sandpaper. **Ask an adult** to help you cut a piece of wood into a square about 2 1/2 in on each side. Then drill a 1/16-in hole through the center of the square.

Make one side of the wood very smooth by rubbing it with fine sandpaper. The lower edges and corners of the wooden square should be rounded and smoothed with sandpaper, too. Fasten the spool to the unsanded side of the square with glue. The holes in the spool and wooden square should line up.

After the glue has dried, attach an inflated balloon to the spool. Air will pass out of the balloon and through the hole in the spool and wood forming a thin layer of air beneath the wood. This thin air layer reduces the friction between the wood and the surface across which it moves.

Place the air car on a smooth surface such as a formica-covered counter. Give it a small push and watch it go. Does it show any sign of slowing down? What happens to the car when the balloon is empty? How does this moving air car illustrate Newton's first law of motion?

If you have access to an air hockey table, you can experiment there, too. Why do the pucks move at constant speed across the table? What happens to them when the air pump is turned off?

Seat belts are a practical application of the first law of motion. To see why, place a doll on a large toy truck. Give the doll and truck a push along a level floor. Arrange for the truck to slam into a pile of bricks. What happens to the doll when the truck collides with the bricks? Now, attach the doll to the truck with a strong rubber band. The rubber band represents a seat belt. Repeat the experiment. What happens to the doll this time? How are seat belts related to the first law of motion? How do they save lives?

There is a second part to Newton's first law. Suppose an object is at rest. It has a speed of zero. Newton's law says it will retain that speed unless acted upon by an outside force. In other words, a body maintains its state of motion, rest, or velocity, unless a force is applied to it. Things tend to stay the way they are. They resist any attempt to change their present state of motion. That's why the first law of motion is often referred to as the law of inertia (resistance to change).

A magician pulling a tablecloth from beneath dishes illustrates inertia. If the frictional forces between the cloth and dishes are small, and the cloth is pulled quickly so that the forces act for a very short time, the dishes will remain in place. You can try the old tablecloth-and-dishes trick for yourself, but use plastic dishes and protective goggles until you become an expert. Place a smooth cloth or several sheets of newspaper on a small table. Set the table with plastic ware, including a cup of water. Give the cover a quick yank and the dishes will remain in place. Be sure to pull the cover straight out, do not yank it upward.

To do a simpler version of the tablecloth trick, cut an index card in half and center it over the mouth of a soda bottle. Place a marble on the card so that it is above the opening in the bottle. Give the card a sharp blow with a snap of your fingers. What happens to the card? What happens to the marble?

Experiment 3.2*

WHEN FORCES ACT

To do this experiment you will need:

- ✔ air car from Experiment 3.1
- ✔ smooth table
- ✔ blocks
- ✔ ball
- ✔ yardstick
- ✔ tape
- ✔ level hallway or gymnasium
- ✔ wagon or skateboard
- ✔ a partner
- ✔ spring scale

As you have seen, an object left alone does not change its state of motion. It will either remain at rest or keep on moving unless a force acts on it. But what happens when a force does act? To find out, place the air car you made in Experiment 3.1 on a smooth ramp. If you have a smooth table, you can make a ramp by placing blocks under the legs to raise one end of the table. Inflate the balloon and place the air car at the top of the ramp. When you release the car, the force of gravity acting along the ramp will be unopposed.

What happens to the car when you release it? Does its speed change? An increase in speed is called acceleration. Does the air car accelerate?

If you drop a ball, gravity will pull it straight toward the center of Earth. Do you think the ball will accelerate? If it falls at a constant speed, how will the time to fall 1 yard compare with the time to fall 2 yards? To fall 4 yards?

To measure the time the ball falls, count to five as fast as you can. You will find it takes just about one second to say, "One, two, three, four, five," as fast as you can. If you get to three when the ball hits the floor, it fell for 3/5 of a second. If you count to five and then get to two on your second count, the ball fell for 1 2/5 seconds.

Drop a ball several times from heights of 1, 2, and 4 yards. Measure the time by the count method for each trial. Does a ball fall at a steady speed under the force of gravity? Or does it accelerate as the air car did?

What happens to a body when a force other than gravity acts on it? Will it accelerate as the air car and ball did? To find out, place pieces of tape at different distances from a starting position along a long, level hallway or gymnasium. The starting position should be marked 0. Then place markers at 5 yards, 10 yards, 15 yards, and at farther points if possible.

You know that if an object moves at constant speed, it will take twice as long to go 20 yards as it will to go 10 yards. On the other hand, if an object accelerates, it takes less than twice as long to go twice as far.

To see what happens when a force unrelated to gravity is applied to a body, have someone sit in a wagon or on a skateboard. Have that person hold one end of a spring scale firmly as shown in Figure 14. Find the force that is needed to just keep the wagon or skateboard moving at a very slow speed. This is the force needed to overcome friction between the wheels and the floor.

Place the vehicle at the 0 position of your marked hallway. Have another person hold the skateboard or wagon. The person on the wagon or skateboard should hold the spring scale firmly as before. Meanwhile, you pull on the other end of the spring scale until you are applying a force greater than friction. You must keep the force constant as you pull the wagon along the hallway after the wagon or skateboard is released. You may have to experiment a few

FIGURE 14

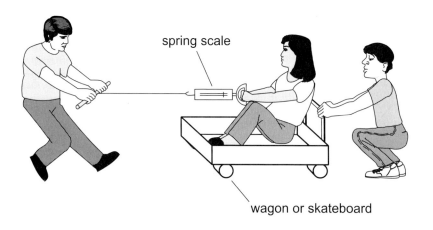

spring scale

wagon or skateboard

times to find a force that you can keep constant all the way along the measured path.

Measure the time it takes to go the various distances. Does the wagon accelerate when a force is applied?

What happens to the acceleration if you make the force larger?

What happens to the acceleration if the same force is applied to someone much heavier sitting on the wagon or skateboard? What happens if a much smaller person is pulled along the path with the same force?

Newton and the Second Law of Motion

Newton found that when any kind of force acts on an object, the object accelerates in the direction of the force. Since gravity acts toward the center of Earth, objects fall downward when released above the ground.

Of course, the force has to be greater than any force opposing the motion such as friction. If a force of 10 pounds is applied to an object and there is a frictional force of 4 pounds, only 6 pounds of force, the net force, will cause acceleration. The other 4 pounds is required to balance friction. In your experiment, if you applied 4 pounds of force just to keep the wagon moving at a constant speed, then the frictional force between wheels and floor was 4 pounds.

Newton found if he doubled the net force acting on a body, the acceleration doubled, too. He discovered that if he doubled the mass, he had to double the net force to have the same acceleration. If he kept the net force constant and doubled the mass, the acceleration was halved. To summarize his results, we can say that the net force applied to a body is proportional to the mass times the acceleration:

$$F = ma \text{ (force = mass x acceleration), or}$$
$$a = F/m \text{ (acceleration = force ÷ mass).}$$

Experiment 3.4

GRAVITY AND MASS

To do this experiment you will need:

- ✔ 2 balls with different masses, such as tennis ball and baseball, or clay
- ✔ book
- ✔ sheet of paper
- ✔ Ping-Pong ball
- ✔ golf ball
- ✔ an ADULT

Find two balls that have different masses. You might use a tennis ball and a baseball, or large and small lumps of clay. The ball that feels heavier has more mass.

Newton reasoned that the gravitational force Earth exerted on bodies near its surface was proportional to their mass, the amount of matter in the body. If body A has twice the mass of body B, the force of gravity on A will be twice that on B. If the mass doubles, and the force doubles too, the acceleration of both bodies should be the same since $a = F/m$.

To test Newton's idea, hold the two balls or lumps of clay at the same height above the floor. Release them together. Do they both strike the floor at the same time? Do they have the same acceleration?

To test the acceleration of two very different masses, hold a book several feet above the floor. The book's cover should be parallel to the floor. Place a sheet of paper that is smaller than the book on its cover. Release the book from both hands at the same time. Does the paper fall with the same acceleration as the book?

If you hold the book in one hand and the paper in the other, do they fall with the same acceleration when you release them? They would if they were dropped in a vacuum, but in air, the resistance of the air retards the paper more than the book. Wad the sheet of paper into a small ball and drop it beside the book. Do they fall together now?

Try a Ping-Pong ball and a golf ball. **Ask an adult** to help you by simultaneously dropping a golf ball and a Ping-Pong ball from a second-story window. You can watch from the ground. Which ball has the greater acceleration? Why?

On one Apollo mission to the Moon, an astronaut dropped a hammer and a feather at the same time while standing on the Moon's surface. A camera recorded their side-by-side motion as they fell to the lunar surface. Though they fell with the same acceleration, the acceleration was only one sixth of the acceleration of falling bodies on Earth. Objects falling near Earth's surface have an acceleration six times greater than objects falling near the

Moon's surface. The Moon's gravity is weaker than Earth's because it has less mass.

Newton was able to show that the force of gravity between two masses is proportional to the masses of both bodies. Double the mass of either, and the force of attraction doubles. Double the mass of both, and the force will be four times as large. But if the distance between the centers of the masses doubles, the force is only one quarter as large. If the distance between the masses is halved, the force quadruples.

Earth's mass is about 82 times that of the Moon. So on the score of mass, our gravity should be 82 times as big as the Moon's. However, the radius of Earth is about 3.7 times as large as the Moon's. So on the score of distance, Earth's gravity, if it had the same mass as the Moon, would be 1/13 as big as the Moon's. When you multiply 82 by 1/13, you get pretty close to 6.

Experiment 3.5

NEWTON AND THE THIRD LAW OF MOTION

To do this experiment you will need:

- ✔ rubber band
- ✔ a partner
- ✔ 2 identical spring scales
- ✔ 2 skateboards or roller skates
- ✔ smooth level floor surface
- ✔ 2 toy trucks
- ✔ clothespin
- ✔ tape

Put a rubber band around your two index fingers. Now stretch the rubber band. How do the forces on each finger compare?

Have a friend hold one spring scale while you hold an identical one that is attached to the one your friend holds. Tell your friend to hold his or her spring scale still while you pull on the other one. How does the force that you exert on your friend compare with the force that your friend exerts on you?

If you can find two skateboards, have a friend sit on one while you sit on the other. Both skateboards should be on a smooth level surface in a hallway, gymnasium, or large room. (If you cannot find skateboards, this experiment can be done on roller skates, or on ice skates.) Sit behind your friend with both skateboards pointed in the same direction. Give your friend a fairly good push with your hands. Does your friend move? Which way does he or she go? Did you move? Which way did you go?

The same experiment can be done on a smaller scale using a pair of toy trucks and a clothespin as shown in Figure 15. Tape the clothespin to one of the trucks. Push the trucks together extending the spring in the clothespin. What happens when you release the trucks and the spring contracts? If you add mass to one truck, how does that affect the results of the experiment?

The experiments you have just done illustrate Newton's third law of motion: When one body exerts a force on a second, the second exerts an equal but opposite force on the first.

FIGURE 15

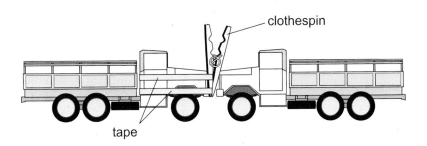

clothespin

tape

You pushed on your friend who accelerated away from you. Your friend, in turn, without even trying, exerted an equal but opposite force on you. Consequently, you accelerated in the opposite direction.

If you repeat the experiment with someone who has much less mass than you do, what do you think will happen? What will happen if your partner is more massive than you?

Do the experiment again, but this time push against a wall. It is clear there is a force on you because you accelerate away from the wall. But where is the opposite force—the one you exerted on the wall? The wall is attached to Earth; when you push on the wall, you are pushing on Earth. Because Earth's mass is huge compared to yours, its acceleration is too small to be observed. The same is true when you release a ball that falls to the ground. Earth pulls on the ball and it accelerates downward. But the ball pulls Earth upward. However, the mass of Earth is so large that its acceleration cannot be detected.

Experiment 3.6

MOTION AND MOMENTUM

To do this experiment you will need:

> ✔ 2 ADULTS
> ✔ long, wide, flat board
> ✔ wooden dowels
> ✔ level floor

All motion involves Newton's third law. When you walk, you push backward against the ground. The ground pushes back on you but in the opposite direction. Therefore, you move forward. Earth, in turn, moves backward, but its mass is so large that we do not see its tiny movement.

Ask an adult to help you set up this experiment. It will convince you that you do push Earth opposite to the direction you walk. Place a long, wide, flat board on a number of rollers, such as wooden dowels, that rest on a level floor. Have two adults, one on each side of you, hold your arms as you try to walk along the board. You will find the board moves backward as you try to walk forward. If you've ever tried to step onto a dock from a boat that wasn't tied to the dock, you've had a similar experience. As you stepped toward the dock, the boat moved away from the dock leaving you, perhaps, in the water.

As you walked along the flat board, pushing backward on it, it pushed forward on you. You moved forward; it moved backward. Both you and the board acquired *momentum*. The momentum of a body is defined as its mass times its velocity. You acquire momentum because you accelerate to a certain speed while a force is applied to you. When you walked on the board, the board pushed you forward as you pushed it backward. As long as you push on it, it pushes back with an equal and opposite force. Therefore, both you and the board acquire equal but opposite momenta. If you and the board have the same mass, you will move in opposite directions but with the same speed. If the board is half as massive as you, it will move twice as fast as you, so that your momentum still will be equal but opposite to the board's. Therefore, the sum of the two momenta will be zero.

$$2m \times v/2 + (-mv) = 0$$

Momentum is always conserved; that is, the total momentum never changes. For you to acquire momentum in one direction, you have to give something else an equal momentum in the opposite direction. You do that by exerting a force on that something else for some time. It exerts an equal but opposite force on you for the same time.

Experiment 3.7

PROJECTILES AND SATELLITES

To do this experiment you will need:

✔ 2 coins	✔ marble
✔ table	✔ block
✔ grooved plastic ruler	✔ tacks
✔ tape	✔ wooden board
✔ sheet of paper	✔ box
✔ carbon paper	

If you lift a ball and release it, it accelerates toward the center of Earth because of the force of gravity. But suppose you throw the ball horizontally, will it still accelerate toward the ground in the same way? To find out, place a coin near the edge of a table. Place a second coin on the end of a ruler as shown in Figure 16. If you hit the ruler sharply at point F while holding the center of the ruler at point M with your fingertip, the ruler will swing about your fingertip. The coin at the table's edge will fly off in a horizontal direction. At the same time, the coin on the end of the ruler will fall straight to

FIGURE 16

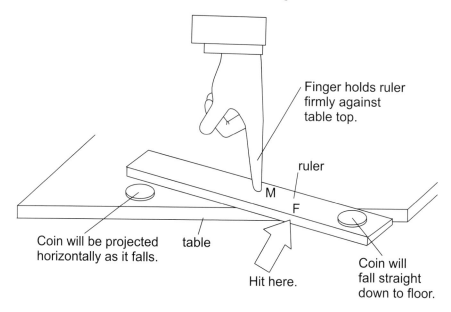

Finger holds ruler firmly against table top.

ruler

M

F

Coin will be projected horizontally as it falls.

table

Hit here.

Coin will fall straight down to floor.

the floor. Listen carefully! Do you hear one sound or two when the coins strike the floor? What does this tell you about the downward acceleration of the two coins? About the downward acceleration of a ball that is thrown horizontally?

You've seen that an object's acceleration toward Earth is the same whether it falls straight down or travels horizontally as it falls. To see how its speed affects the path of a ball launched horizontally, build a ramp like the one shown in Figure 17. Tape a long sheet of paper on the floor beneath the ramp. Cover the paper with a sheet of carbon paper to mark the point where a marble lands when it falls from the end of the ramp. To give the marble some horizontal speed when it reaches the end of the ruler, release it from various points (A, B, C, D) along the ramp. As you see, the higher the point from which it is released, the faster will be its horizontal speed when it leaves the ruler. Mark the landing points of the marble as its horizontal speed increases. How does its horizontal speed affect its flight path?

Newton realized that if an object could be launched horizontally from a very high point above Earth, where air resistance was negligible, its path would become longer and

FIGURE 17

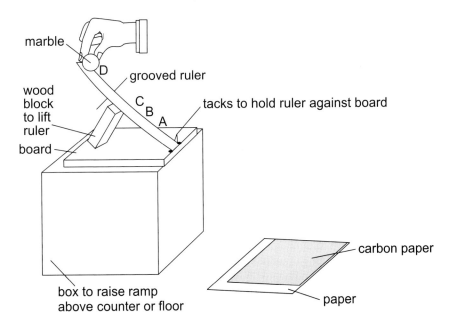

FIGURE 18

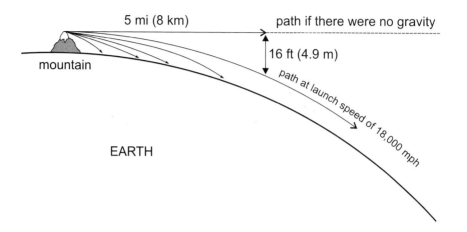

5 mi (8 km) path if there were no gravity

16 ft (4.9 m)

mountain

path at launch speed of 18,000 mph

EARTH

longer as its speed was increased. Finally, at a speed of about 29,000 km/hr (18,000 mph), the object's rate of fall would match the curvature of Earth as shown in Figure 18. Earth's surface curves 4.9 m (16 ft) for every 8 km (5 mi) of horizontal distance. Thus, since an object falls off its horizontal path 4.9 m/s (16 ft/s), its path will match Earth's curvature if it is traveling with a horizontal speed of 5 mi/s (29,000 km/hr or 18,000 mph).

Newton knew how to put satellites into orbit about Earth. *Sputnik* would have been no surprise to him. What Newton lacked was the technology to accelerate objects to speeds of 29,000 km/hr.

ROCKETS AND SATELLITES

To do this experiment you will need:

✔ soda straw	✔ tape
✔ balloon	✔ thread

Rockets used to send satellites into orbit use the principle of momentum to develop the necessary speed of 29,000 km/hr (18,000 mph). By pushing fuel out the back of the rocket at high speed, the rocket acquires an equal momentum in the opposite direction.

You can make a simple rocket as shown in Figure 19. Tape a soda straw to a balloon, preferably an oblong one, and mount the soda straw on a long thread. When you release the balloon, the air pushed out of the balloon's neck will provide an equal force on the balloon. The momentum to the rear acquired by the air will equal the forward momentum supplied to the balloon rocket.

In principle, all rockets operate in this manner. However, the mass and speed of a satellite is much greater than the momentum of

FIGURE 19

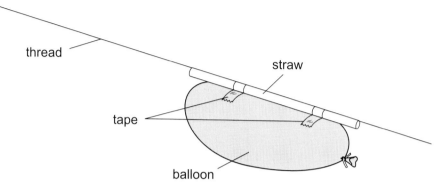

thread

straw

tape

balloon

the balloon you launched. Fuels that can provide lots of momentum must be used to send satellites into orbit.

Little was done to develop the technology needed to launch the satellites that Newton knew were possible until Robert H. Goddard began building rockets in the 1920s. Goddard used gasoline to fuel his first rockets, but he realized that once rockets left Earth's atmosphere and entered space, they would have to carry their own oxygen to burn the fuel.

People laughed at Goddard because they heard he was building a spaceship to go to the Moon. But Charles Lindbergh recognized the significance of Goddard's research and helped him find financial support. During the 1930s, Goddard patented the idea of multistage rockets. He realized that it was foolish to lift the entire rocket into space. So he designed rockets in stages. Once the fuel in each stage had been used, that part of the rocket would fall back to Earth. By using stages, less fuel is needed because the mass being lifted is reduced after each stage. This principle of multistaging is still used in rockets today. The space shuttle discards its solid-fuel rocket boosters and its external fuel tank as it ascends into orbit.

As Goddard anticipated, the space shuttle carries its own supply of oxygen into space. The oxygen is in a liquid state under very high pressure. It is used to combine with liquid hydrogen. The reason for choosing hydrogen as the fuel is simple. Hydrogen is the lightest gas known and it produces the most energy per mass of any fuel. By burning hydrogen, the mass of the fuel lifted is as small as it can be. And the burned fuel leaves the rocket engine with the greatest momentum possible providing the shuttle with an equal momentum in the opposite direction.

4

ROUND AND ROUND WE GO

Since the weather satellite *Tiros 1* was launched on April 1, 1960, meteorologists have been able to base their predictions on weather systems that they can see on a global scale. Most television weather reports include satellite photographs of the clouds and weather systems over the entire country. In addition to visible cloud cover, weather satellites provide meteorologists with information about soil moisture, atmospheric temperatures, ozone levels, gas and aerosol concentrations, and rainfall over the oceans.

Other satellites take photographs that enable scientists to prepare maps of unexplored areas; analyze forest, mineral, soil, and water resources; and make crop and earthquake forecasts. Communication satellites make it possible to send television, radio, and telephone signals from one continent to another. Since 1964 we have been able to transmit television broadcasts of Olympic Games and other events of worldwide interest across the globe so they can be viewed live.

Earth Is a Sphere

People have known for centuries that Earth is round, but the spectacular views from satellites, and especially from the Moon, should convince even members of the Flat Earth Society that Earth is a sphere.

Early evidence about the shape of Earth was more subtle. For example, during an eclipse of the Moon, Earth's shadow as it crosses the Moon was seen to be curved. As early as the fourth century B.C., Eratosthenes estimated the radius of Earth. He knew that on the first day of summer, the Sun was directly overhead in the city of Syene (now Aswân). He knew this because the image of the Sun could be seen reflected from the water in a deep well in Syene on that day. Eratosthenes lived in Alexandria, which was 500 miles due north of Syene. At noon, on the first day of summer, when he knew the Sun was directly overhead in Syene, he measured the shadow of a tall pillar in Alexandria. He found the Sun's rays made an angle of 7.5 degrees with the pillar. He reasoned, as you can see in Figure 20, that if the Sun's rays are parallel, then 500 miles is equivalent to 7.5 degrees of Earth's 360 degrees. Each 1,000 miles then is equivalent to 15 degrees. Since $360°/15° = 24$, the entire circumference of Earth must be 24,000 miles. Its diameter is 24,000 miles divided by pi (π). To calculate the diameter of any circle, you divide its circumference by pi. Pi is approximately 3.14. Hence, Earth's diameter is about 8,000 miles; its radius 4,000 miles.

Early sailors knew that the altitude of the North Star decreased as they sailed south. Once they sailed south of the equator, Polaris dropped below the horizon. Such observations can be explained if Earth is a sphere. In fact, as you saw from Figure 1, the altitude of the North Star will be equal to the latitude from which it is viewed.

By the eighteenth century, educated people believed the Sun, Moon, and stars appeared to move across the sky because Earth rotated on

FIGURE 20

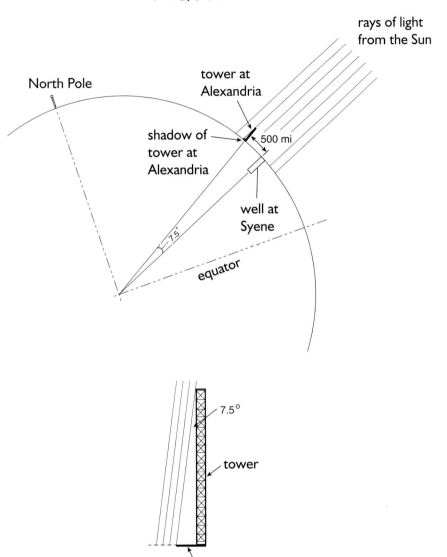

rays of light
from the Sun

North Pole

tower at
Alexandria

shadow of
tower at
Alexandria

500 mi

well at
Syene

7.5

equator

7.5°

tower

shadow

its axis once each day. But direct evidence of Earth's rotation was not available before the middle of the nineteenth century, when Jean Foucault built his famous pendulum. A Foucault pendulum consists of a heavy metal bob suspended from a very long string. You may have seen one in a science museum.

Because a pendulum will maintain its direction of swing (Newton's first law of motion), Foucault knew, when he saw the pendulum change its direction of swing, that Earth must be rotating.

Experiment 4.1

FOUCAULT'S PENDULUM

To do this experiment you will need:

✔ clamp   ✔ clay

✔ string   ✔ turntable

✔ metal sinker

To make a model of a Foucault pendulum, hang a pendulum over a turntable. Pretend that the center of the turntable is the North Pole and set the pendulum swinging as shown in Figure 21. You will see that the pendulum maintains the direction or plane of its swing. If a Foucault pendulum is swinging above the North Pole, its direction of swing will appear to rotate through 360 degrees every 24 hours. To see why this happens, put a piece of clay on the turntable to represent you. Then slowly turn the turntable while the pendulum is swinging. As you can see, the direction of its swing appears to rotate relative to the clay.

FIGURE 21

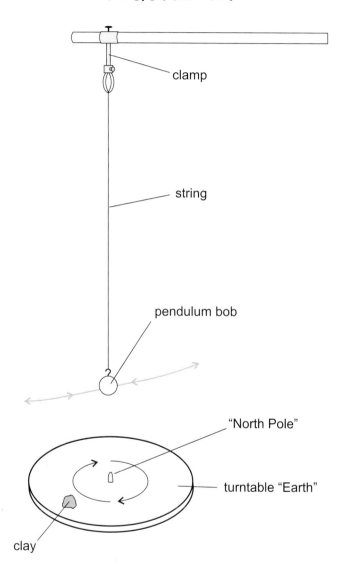

clamp

string

pendulum bob

"North Pole"

turntable "Earth"

clay

Experiment 4.2

KEEPING SATELLITES ALOFT

To do this experiment you will need:

✔ marble   ✔ rigid plastic cake cover

When a satellite is launched, it acquires momentum from the rocket fuel used to increase its speed to the 29,000 km/hr (18,000 mph) required for orbit. The exact path of a satellite is controlled by a complex guidance system. Radio signals sent from a control center activate sensors on the satellite that feed data into computers that automatically adjust the direction of the vehicle and keep it on a preplanned path to orbit. If you have a remote-controlled toy car or airplane, you are familiar with a simple guidance system.

Once a satellite is in orbit, no fuel is required to keep it there. You know from Newton's first law that a body in motion will maintain its motion unless a force acts on it. In the case of a satellite, there is a force—the force of gravity. Earth's pull on the satellite causes it to fall toward Earth just like any other body. But by the time it reaches orbit, the satellite has a speed of 5 mi/s (18,000 mph) along its orbit. The combination of its sideways speed and its acceleration toward Earth gives it a path that matches Earth's curved surface as you saw in Chapter 3.

If the force on a satellite suddenly disappeared, what would its path be? To find out, put a marble inside a rigid plastic cake cover. Gently swirl the cake cover on a level surface so that the marble follows a circular path along the inside circumference of the cover. Once the marble "satellite" is in orbit, lift one side of the cake cover. What path does the marble satellite take? Does it continue to move in a circle? Does it fly outward? Or does it move in a straight line tangent to the circle?

Any object moving in a circular path is accelerating toward the center of the circle because there is a force pulling it inward. This inward force is called a centripetal force. In the case of a satellite, gravity provides the centripetal force. If you tie a ball to the end of a string and swing it around your head, you have to pull inward on the string to make the ball move in a circle. When a car goes around a curve, the tires push outward against the road. The road, in turn, pushes inward on the tires supplying the centripetal force needed to make the car go in a circle.

If the road is covered with ice, no centripetal force may be available. As a result, the car will continue to move in a straight line, which may carry it off the highway, just like the marble released from the cake cover.

Experiment 4.3

AN ACCELEROMETER

To do this experiment you will need:

✔ tall, narrow plastic vial with lid	✔ warm water
✔ soap	✔ clay
	✔ turntable

An accelerometer is a device that allows you to detect acceleration. If you have a small carpenter's level, you can use it as an accelerometer. If not, you can make one.

Find a tall, narrow plastic vial. Put a tiny piece of soap in the bottom of the vial. Then pour warm water into the vessel. Leave a little space at the top so a small bubble will be present after you close the vial.

Hold the vial in a horizontal, level position. Then accelerate the vial forward. You will see the bubble move in the direction of the acceleration. As the vial slows down and comes to rest, the bubble will move toward the rear of the vial, which is the direction of the acceleration when the vial decelerates.

An Inward Acceleration

To convince yourself that there is an inward or centripetal acceleration on an object moving in a circle, use some clay to fasten an accelerometer to a turntable as shown in Figure 22. Be sure the bubble is in the center of the vial. What happens to the bubble when the turntable is spinning? What is the direction of the acceleration when the accelerometer moves in a circle? What happens to the size of the acceleration when the turntable spins faster? When it spins slower? How can you tell?

If you've ever played snap-the-whip, you know that you move faster as you get farther from the center of a circle. The same is true on a merry-go-round or a turntable. To see how the

FIGURE 22

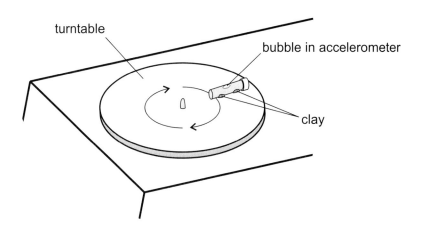

turntable

bubble in accelerometer

clay

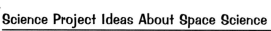

inward acceleration is related to the distance from the center, move the accelerometer closer to the center of the turntable. What do you find?

What do you predict the inward acceleration will be if you place the bubble right over the center of the turntable? Were you right?

Experiment 4.4

MEASURING CENTRIPETAL FORCES

To do this experiment you will need:

✔ 2 rubber stoppers

✔ ballpoint pen

✔ thin nylon string, 2 m (6 ft) long

✔ 2 paper clips

✔ several identical metal washers

✔ stopwatch, or watch with a second hand

✔ tape

To see how mass, radius, and period are related to the centripetal force needed to keep a satellite in orbit, you can build the apparatus shown in Figure 23. You can use a rubber stopper to represent a satellite. The weight of washers suspended from a string attached to the "satellite" supply the centripetal force.

Take a ballpoint pen apart. After you have removed the ink cartridge, you can use the barrel of the pen to swing the "satellite" as shown in Figure 23. Thread a strong piece of thin nylon string, about 2 m (6 ft) long, through the barrel of the pen. Use the smoother end of the barrel as the upper end around which the

FIGURE 23

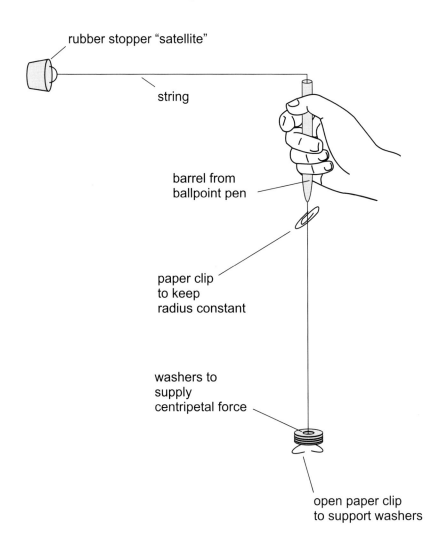

rubber stopper "satellite"

string

barrel from
ballpoint pen

paper clip
to keep
radius constant

washers to
supply
centripetal force

open paper clip
to support washers

string will move in a circle. The lower end of the string can be tied to a paper clip that will support a number of identical metal washers. The weight of these washers provides the centripetal force needed to make the satellite move along a circular orbit.

Arrange the satellite so that its center is about 1 m (3 ft) from the top of the pen barrel. Another paper clip can be attached to the string about 2.5 cm (1 in) below the barrel. When you swing the satellite in its orbit, keep this paper clip about 2.5 cm (1 in) below the barrel so you can be sure that the radius of the orbit does not change. When you have the satellite moving smoothly at a radius of 1 m (3 ft), count the number of revolutions made by the satellite in 30 seconds. (A revolution is one time around the circular orbit.) The time required for the satellite to make one revolution is its period. You can find the period by dividing 30 seconds by the number of revolutions you counted. What is the period of your satellite? Why is it better to measure the time for many revolutions rather than just one?

What is the period of your satellite if you double the centripetal force but keep the radius the same? You can double the force by doubling the number of washers at the bottom of the string. How would you make the centripetal force four times as big? How much force is needed to halve the satellite's period?

If you halve the radius of the orbit, what force is needed to keep the period the same? One guess might be that at half the radius only half as much force would be required. Try it! Was it a good guess?

From Newton's second law, you might reason that doubling the mass of the satellite would require twice as much force to keep the satellite moving along the same orbit with the same period. Tape or tie another identical rubber stopper to the first one to double the mass of the satellite. With the same orbital radius of 1 m (3 ft), does the period remain about the same when you double the centripetal force acting on twice the mass?

Experiment 4.5

EXPERIENCING G-FORCES

To do this experiment you will need:

- ✔ portable bathroom scale
- ✔ elevator
- ✔ an ADULT

When you jump from a diving board into water, gravity causes you to accelerate at 32 feet per second per second. When you stand on the floor, the floor pushes up on you with a force equal to your weight. You feel what is called a 1 g-force. If you were accelerated along a track in a rocket sled at twice the acceleration that gravity provides, you would feel 2 g-forces on your back. In other words, you would feel as if your weight had suddenly doubled.

To experience at least a partial increase in weight, take a portable bathroom scale into an elevator, **with an adult to accompany you**. Stand on the scale and press the button for an upper floor. What happens to your weight, as recorded on the scale, when the elevator accelerates upward? What is your weight when the elevator moves at a steady speed? What happens to your weight as the elevator decelerates before coming to a stop? Can you predict what will happen to your weight when, after coming to a stop, you press the button for a lower floor?

Of course, you are no heavier or lighter in an elevator than anywhere else. But the forces causing you to accelerate make you feel heavier because you push back with an equal force. If the elevator accelerates downward, it does not push as hard on you; therefore, you cannot push as hard on it, and so the force you exert on the scales resting on the elevator floor decreases.

The g-forces you experience in an elevator are quite small. If you ride a roller coaster or some of the other rides at an amusement park, you will experience larger g-forces. These forces will make you feel very heavy for short periods of time. In one of these rides, the force lasts longer. People stand against the wall of a huge barrel that can be made to spin. When it is spinning at full speed, the bottom of the barrel is lowered, but no one falls. The barrel is spinning so fast that the centripetal force exerted by the walls on the people to keep them going in a circle holds them firmly in place.

You will find it interesting and fun to take your accelerometer with you to an amusement park. Are you able to predict the direction of the acceleration on these rides?

LOOP-THE-LOOP

To do this experiment you will need:

✔ quart of water	✔ plastic pail

In a loop-the-loop roller coaster, the cars stay on the tracks even when they are upside down. The centripetal force the tracks exert on the cars is greater than the force of gravity. Therefore, the inward acceleration of the cars (and the people in them) toward the center of the loop is greater than the acceleration due to gravity. As a result, the cars do not fall from the track. If the diameter of the loop is 12 m (40 ft), the cars only have to move at a speed of 29 km/hr (18 mph) at the top of the loop to stay on the track. Since the cars are moving much faster than that, there is no danger of their falling. In fact, when you are on the ride, you will feel a force on the seat of your pants even when you are upside down.

You can see the same "loop-the-loop" effect in an experiment you can do outdoors. Place about a quart of water in a plastic pail and swing it in a vertical circle. Even when the moving pail is upside down, water will not spill. The bottom of the pail has a centripetal acceleration that is greater than the acceleration due to gravity. If you are wearing your bathing suit, slow down the pail to see how slowly the pail must revolve before water spills out.

On Board a Satellite

As you have seen with your rubber-stopper satellite, twice as much centripetal force is needed to keep a satellite with twice as much mass moving along the same orbit at the same speed. With real satellites this happens naturally. Doubling the mass of a satellite, doubles its weight (the gravitational force exerted by Earth).

To double the rubber-stopper satellite's period along the same orbit, the force must be made one quarter as big. With real satellites, the force can be made smaller by placing the satellite farther from Earth. If the satellite is about 5.5 Earth radii above Earth's surface, its period will be 24 hours. At this altitude the satellite has the same period as Earth. Do you see why communication satellites are placed at this altitude?

With real satellites, the force on the satellite is the force of gravity. As a result, the satellite and everything on it falls toward Earth at the same rate. If you were riding on a satellite, it would be similar to riding on a free-falling elevator, there would be no force on your feet. You would feel weightless.

You experience the sensation of feeling weightless when you jump off a diving board into water. The feeling does not last long because you soon hit the water. You've probably experienced partial weightlessness on an elevator as it starts to descend. You can also experience weightlessness on a playground swing. If you are swinging high, you will feel weightless at the peak of your swing. At the moment the swing stops and starts its descent, both you and the swing will be falling at the same rate. You will feel no pressure between your seat and the seat of the swing for a short time. As you descend along the circular path, you feel the swing pushing on you because it must provide the centripetal force needed to move you along a circular path.

During their training, astronauts experience weightlessness by flying in airplanes that make long humplike arcs through the air. The planes fly at such a speed that the centripetal acceleration along their curved paths matches the acceleration due to gravity. As a result, the plane and all its contents are accelerating toward Earth at the same rate as any falling object. Sometimes, you will experience this same effect when you go over an unexpected bump in a car.

<u>5</u>

LIFE IN SPACE

Living in space is very different from living on Earth. Even the view is different. On Earth you see a blue sky and red sunsets. In space the sky is black and the Sun remains yellow as long as it is visible.

The sky appears blue because of Earth's atmosphere. The oxygen and nitrogen gases that make up the atmosphere absorb and emit light—a process called scattering. Because these gases tend to scatter the shorter wavelengths of

FIGURE 24

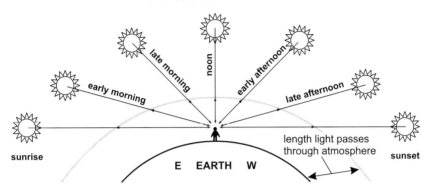

light (blue) more than longer wavelengths (red), and because the scattered light is emitted in all directions, the sky appears blue. In space, where there is no atmosphere, light is not scattered. As a result, we can see light coming from stars, but the space around the stars appears black because there is nothing in the vacuum of space to scatter light.

On Earth, as the Sun approaches the horizon, sunlight must travel through a greater length of atmosphere as you can see from Figure 24. Because sunlight encounters more and more gas as it sinks toward the horizon, more and more of the light at the blue end of the spectrum is scattered. The light that is least scattered is red. Hence, the setting Sun appears redder and redder as it approaches the horizon because only reddish light from the Sun comes through the air.

Experiment 5.1

BLUE SKIES AND RED SUNSETS

To do this experiment you will need:

✔ slide projector

✔ tank of water

✔ powdered milk or nondairy creamer

You can make a model sunset and see the blue "sky" caused by scattered light as well. In a dark room, shine the light from a slide projector through a tank full of water. To scatter light, add a small amount of powdered milk or a nondairy creamer to the water and stir. Notice how the water around the light coming through the water begins to take on a bluish color. Continue adding small amounts of the powder and stirring. What happens to the color of the light coming through the water directly from the light?

Life in a Weightless Environment

It is difficult to imagine the feeling of weightlessness. You can get a sense of what it would be like by floating in water. However, you can swim in water; you cannot "swim" if you are stranded in the center of a space station. There is nothing to push against. If you were to find yourself on the ship's surface, you might try to walk. But when you push against the floor, you will move away from the floor (a direction we normally call "up") as well as forward. One way to avoid such unwanted motion is to wear shoes with Velcro soles and line the inside of the space ship with the same material. That way, your feet will stick to the surface, and you will not find yourself bouncing off the walls.

What would you do if you were stranded and weightless in the center of a spaceship? This is but one of the many problems you might face in the weightless environment of space. The following activities will introduce you to a few of them.

Experiment 5.2

PRESSURE AND SPACE

To do this experiment you will need:

✔ small nail	✔ tub of water
✔ Styrofoam coffee cup	✔ balloon
✔ water	✔ tie band
✔ sink	✔ small pin

If you have ever dived deep into water, you know that the weight of the water produces a pressure that can exert forces in all directions. To see how the weight of water affects the pressure it can exert, use a small nail to punch three holes in the side of a Styrofoam coffee cup. Make holes near the bottom, top, and middle of the cup's side. Cover the holes with your fingers and fill the cup with water. Hold the cup over a sink and release your fingers. Notice how far the water in each stream is pushed outward. How is the pressure on the water coming out of each hole related to the weight of the water above the hole?

The pressure effect you have just seen is called *hydrostatic pressure*. The higher the column of water, the greater is the pressure at the bottom of the column. The pressure increases with depth because the weight of a tall columnn of water is greater than that of a short column. But would there be hydrostatic pressure in a weightless environment?

To find out, fill the cup with water again. This time, after you remove your fingers from the holes, let the cup fall 6 or more feet into a tub of water. While falling, the cup and its contents will be accelerating at the same rate. It is similar to a weightless environment.

What do you notice about the water streams while the cup is falling? Try it several times to be sure. Would there be hydrostatic pressure on a spaceship?

To create pressure in a spaceship, you would have to provide some force other than weight to move fluids. To see one way this might be done, fill a large, strong balloon with water. Seal the neck of the balloon with a tie band. Use a small pin to make a tiny hole on one side of the balloon. A stream of water, similar to the one you found coming from the side of the coffee cup, will emerge. Now drop the balloon into a tub of water as you did the coffee cup. Repeat the experiment several times to be sure. Does the stream stop flowing this time?

What is one way you could provide the pressure needed to move fluids in a spaceship?

Experiment 5.3

DINING IN SPACE

To do this experiment you will need:

✔ paper cup	✔ chair
✔ water	✔ pen or pencil
✔ straw	✔ paper

Eating in space presents problems. Food will not stay on your plate. If you nudge it with a fork, it will keep moving. Milk will not pour from a glass—it is weightless. You might wonder if you could eat at all in a weightless environment. After all, there is no force to carry the food from mouth to stomach.

Is starvation a natural consequence of weightlessness? To find out, fill a paper cup with water, rest it on the floor, and place a straw in it. Lie on a chair and bend your head down over the water so that your stomach is higher than your mouth. Can you overcome gravity and drink water through the straw when you are in this position? Could you drink and eat if you were weightless?

Astronauts living in the weightlessness of space drink from plastic bottles. Squeezing the bottles with their hands provides the pressure needed to move the liquids into their mouths. Some of the food they eat is also squeezed from plastic bags. The involuntary contraction of muscles in the esophagus moves food and liquids from mouth to stomach.

Sticky foods can be served on plates fastened to a table, but care must be taken not to move spoons and forks too fast or the food may keep on moving when the silverware stops. Have you ever seen astronauts with egg on their faces because they forgot the first law of motion?

Imagine preparing and eating a meal in a spaceship. Compare such a meal with one on Earth. List all the precautions you would have to take and all the things you would have to do differently if you were eating in space.

You can eat and drink in space, but the food does not have much taste. In weightless conditions, body fluids do not tend to drain into your legs. As a result, your face appears fatter and you have a runny nose and more fluid in your chest—all the symptoms of a cold, the same symptoms that make it difficult to taste and smell.

Experiment 5.4

CONVECTION AND SPACE

To do this experiment you will need:

- ✔ graduated cylinder or measuring cup
- ✔ water
- ✔ balance scale
- ✔ glass
- ✔ cooking oil
- ✔ cup
- ✔ 2 medicine vials
- ✔ cold water
- ✔ food coloring
- ✔ hot tap water
- ✔ eyedropper

You can eat in space, but not by candlelight. When a candle burns on Earth, the hot gases produced from the burning wax rise as cooler, denser air moves in around the candle forcing the hot, lighter gases upward.

A hot gas weighs less than an equal volume of the same gas when it is cool. This is true of liquids as well. Weigh 100 mL of water. Then weigh an equal volume of cooking oil. Which is heavier? Now mix some cooking oil and water in a cup. Which liquid rises to the top?

Fill a medicine vial with cold water. To a second vial add several drops of food coloring. Then fill the second vial with hot tap water. Using an eyedropper, remove some of the colored hot water. Carefully lower the eyedropper into the cold water, and very gently squeeze out a drop of the colored hot water. Does hot water rise or sink in cold water?

Repeat the experiment, but this time color the cold water and gently squeeze it into some clear hot water. Does the cold water rise or sink in the hot water?

In a weightless environment, there is no force to move carbon dioxide and other waste gases from a burning candle. As a result, fresh, cooler, denser, oxygen-laden air will not move in to replace the waste gases. The candle is quickly extinguished by its own carbon dioxide. No fire extinguisher is needed.

Experiment 5.5

A WEIGHTLESS BURNING CANDLE

To do this experiment you will need:

✔ an ADULT	✔ 2 pairs of safety goggles
✔ birthday candle	✔ stepladder
✔ clay	✔ lawn
✔ glass jar with cover	✔ soft pillows, sand, or soft earth
✔ match	
✔ watch or clock with a second hand	

Ask an adult to help you with this experiment. It involves dropping a burning candle.

Place a birthday candle in a small lump of clay on the bottom of a large, wide-mouth glass jar. Have an adult light the candle. Screw the cover onto the jar and measure how long the candle will burn inside the closed jar.

Remove the cover and candle, invert the jar, and move it up and down to get out any gases formed by combustion. When you are sure the jar is filled with fresh air, **have an adult relight the candle** and cover the jar at the top of a stepladder on a lawn. The jar can then be dropped onto some soft pillows or a pile of sand or soft earth. Stand back away from the falling jar and watch the burning candle as it falls. Does it continue to burn, or does it go out?

In doing this experiment, both you and your adult helper should wear protective shielding over your face in case the jar should break! It would also be a good idea to have a fire extinguisher nearby. It is not likely that breakage will occur if the jar falls onto soft pillows, but it is wise to be overly cautious where fire and glass are concerned.

On Earth, differences in density (weight per volume) due to expansions or contractions caused by temperature changes create convection currents. In the weightless environment of a spaceship, nothing sinks or floats so there are no convection currents. To be sure there is fresh air for the astronauts to breathe, a circulating system must constantly force air around the spaceship.

When crystals are grown on Earth, convection currents created by the heat released in the process often produce flaws in the crystals. Companies that grow crystals, such as the silicon crystals used in computers, hope that they will be able to produce better crystals with greater efficiency in space factories where there are no convection currents.

Experiment 5.6

SEDIMENTATION

To do this experiment you will need:

- ✔ mud
- ✔ sand
- ✔ water
- ✔ plastic vial
- ✔ sawdust

Put some mud, sand, and water into a plastic vial. Cover the vial and shake it. Watch the solid matter settle. Which particles seem to settle fastest? Slowest?

The settling of solid particles to the bottom of a liquid is called *sedimentation*—a process commonly used in chemistry to separate mixtures. Would sedimentation occur in a weightless environment?

Repeat the experiment, but this time add sawdust to the mud, water, and sand in the vial. What happens this time after the vial is shaken? Can you explain why some material moves to the top and some to the bottom of the vial?

Chemical reactions that take place between a liquid and substances that are not soluble in the liquid would occur much faster in a space laboratory orbiting Earth. Can you explain why?

Experiment 5.7

GROWING PLANTS IN SPACE

To do this experiment you will need:

✔ paper towel	✔ can
✔ dish	✔ tape
✔ water	✔ small pan
✔ food coloring	✔ celery stalks
✔ scissors	

For plants to grow on Earth, water, carrying dissolved minerals from the soil, must move upward through the roots and stems to the leaves where plants manufacture food. Some believe that plants will grow faster in a weightless environment because the water can move faster along the stems if gravity is not present to retard it.

To check up on this idea, dip a piece of paper towel into some water to which a few drops of food coloring have been added. Notice how water "climbs" up the towel. If you watch this under a microscope, you will see that the water fills the tiny spaces between the wood fibers that make

FIGURE 25

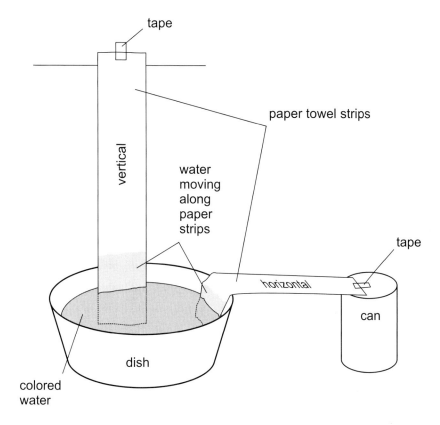

tape

paper towel strips

vertical

water
moving
along
paper
strips

tape

horizontal

can

dish

colored
water

up the towel. There are similar tiny channels in the stems of plants through which water moves. Water is attracted to the walls of these narrow pathways. Because water is cohesive (holds together well), water that is attracted to these walls pulls more water along with it, filling the channels. The movement of liquids upward in small spaces is called *capillary action*.

To see how gravity affects capillary action, set up the experiment shown in Figure 25. Cut two identical strips from a paper towel. Hang one vertically. Lay the other one out horizontally. One end of each strip should rest in a small pan of colored water. Watch the colored water move along the two strips. How far has it moved along each strip after 10 minutes? After 20 minutes? After 1 hour? In which strip does water move faster? Does the movement of the water ever stop in either strip?

You might repeat this experiment using celery stalks in place of paper towel strips. But you may have to cut across the stalks in order to see how far the water has moved.

Do you think water would move faster through plants in a weightless spaceship than through plants growing on Earth?

Experiment 5.8

A BATHROOM IN SPACE

To do this experiment you will need:

✔ 2 balloons	✔ tape
✔ string	

Without gravity how would you take a shower? A pressurized tank could be used to force the water into a stream, but once it hit your body, the droplets would bounce all over the spaceship.

One way to avoid this problem is to use Wash 'n Dri towelettes. Another is to enclose the shower from top to bottom so no water can escape. At the bottom of the shower, low pressure is created in a drain by means of a vacuum pump.

Another way to create low pressure is with fast-moving streams of air. To see how this works, hang two balloons with string from the top of a doorway so they are a few inches apart. Now blow air between the balloons. What happens to the balloons?

If you examine an atomizer, such as the kind used to spray cologne, you will see that it works in a similar way. An airstream is directed across the top of a tube that dips into the liquid. This reduces the pressure at the top of the tube and so cologne is forced up the tube by the higher pressure over the liquid.

In a spaceship, fast-flowing air and water streams under the toilet create a low pressure that causes urine and feces to move into the drains leading to collecting tanks where waste is stored.

Muscles in Space

On Earth, the stresses created by the weight of your flesh as it pulls on the bones of your skeleton in some way cause new bone matter to form replacing any that may disappear through wear and metabolism. But in the weightless confines of space, this does not happen unless an effort is made to maintain muscle tone. Early ventures into space led space scientists to realize that astronauts would have to engage in vigorous daily exercise.

In a zero-g environment, your bones respond in the same way that they do among the bedridden on Earth; they lose calcium and become weaker. Through lack of work, your muscles (including heart muscle) and blood vessels lose their tone. Blood volume, red blood cells, and the salt concentration in your body fluids all diminish. As a result, Charles Conrad, Joseph Kerwin, and Paul Weitz, the first crew aboard *Skylab*, who spent 28 days in space in 1973, were barely able to walk when they returned to Earth. They felt faint because blood tended to pool in their lower body, their heart rates were higher than normal, they had lost weight, and their muscles ached from having to carry their newfound weight.

It was discovered that these effects could be greatly reduced by 90 minutes of vigorous exercise on an ergometer each day. In addition to daily exercise, Russian cosmonauts found that wearing suits with crisscrossing elastic cords improved muscle tone over long periods in space. Every movement required muscular effort. It was uncomfortable, but it helped to prevent the physiological effects of weightlessness.

Experiment 5.9

FINDING YOUR WEIGHT IN SPACE

To do this experiment you will need:

✔ C-clamp	✔ graph paper
✔ yardstick	✔ pencil
✔ bookshelf	✔ watch
✔ 100-g mass	✔ string
✔ tape	✔ stone

During their time in space, astronauts keep records of what they eat, how they feel, their height and weight, and other statistics. But how can they determine their weights in a weightless environment?

Actually, they do not measure their weight; they measure their mass, which is the same everywhere. Since they are weightless, they will not stretch the springs of any scales used to measure weight. Even the equal arm balances used to measure mass in laboratories cannot be used here. Such balances depend on the equal gravitational pull on the masses at either end of the balance. However, there are balances called inertial balances that can be used to measure mass anywhere. Such balances do not depend on gravity for their operation.

The inertial balances used in space stations or space laboratories are large enough for a person to sit in. But you can make and calibrate a small model inertial balance quite easily. Use a C-clamp to fasten a yardstick to the side of a bookshelf as shown in Figure 26a. Fasten a 100-g mass to the end of the yardstick with tape. Then measure the time it takes the yardstick to swing back and forth (oscillate) 50 times. Repeat the process again using heavier masses. Each time, record the mass and the time required for the yardstick to make 50 oscillations. Does the oscillation time of the yardstick depend on the mass attached to the end of the stick?

Plot a graph of the time to make 50 swings versus the mass attached to the yardstick. Plot time on the vertical axis and mass on the horizontal axis. Connect the points you plotted with a smooth line.

Now attach an object of unknown mass to the end of the yardstick. You might use another C-clamp or a stone. Measure the time it takes for the unknown mass to make 50 oscillations. Then use the graph you have made to estimate its mass. If you have a regular balance, you can check the mass of the unknown and see how close your prediction was.

FIGURE 26

a)

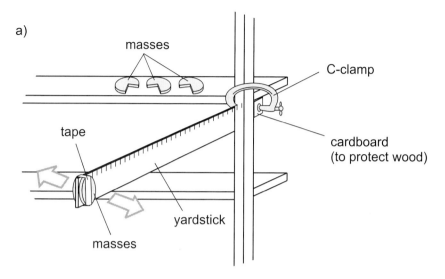

masses

C-clamp

tape

cardboard
(to protect wood)

yardstick

masses

b)

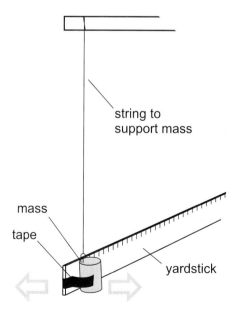

string to
support mass

mass

tape

yardstick

To see that gravity does not enter into this measurement of mass, hang one of the masses you used from a long string so that it does not rest on the yardstick as shown in Figure 26b. Tape it to the yardstick so it will move when the yardstick moves. The mass will now move with the yardstick balance, but it is not exerting any gravitational force on the yardstick. How does the time required to make a certain number of swings now, compared with the time it took to make the same number of swings when the mass was pulling downward on the yardstick?

Experiment 5.10

ENERGY IN SPACE

To do this experiment you will need:

✔ paintbrush	✔ water
✔ flat black paint	✔ thermometer
✔ 4 aluminum pie pans	✔ black ink
✔ cardboard	✔ food coloring
✔ measuring cup	✔ aluminum foil

People living in space have the same energy needs as you. They must stay warm, they need light when they are in Earth's shadow, and they need electricity to run motors, stoves, air-conditioning, etc. The energy required in spaceships comes from the Sun. Giant panels of photovoltaic cells convert sunlight into electricity.

If you can get some photovoltaic cells, you might connect them to a small electric motor and see if you can make the motor run with solar power.

Solar energy can also be used to heat air and water in a spaceship. In fact, sometimes the heat produced can raise temperatures so high that it becomes uncomfortable. Then the problem becomes one of getting rid of excess solar energy.

To see how color affects the conversion of sunlight to heat, paint the inside surface of an aluminum pie pan with flat black paint. Place this pan together with one that has not been painted side by side on a sheet of cardboard in a warm, sunny place. After the paint has dried, pour a cup of water in each pan and leave them in direct sunlight for several hours. Every few minutes use a thermometer to measure the temperature of the water in each pan. In which pan does the water get hotter? Can you explain why?

Repeat the experiment with two more aluminum pans. Add black ink to the water in one pan. Which pan do you predict will get hotter?

You might also place a series of pans side by side and place equal amounts of water in each. Color the water in each pan differently using food coloring. Does the color of the water affect its ability to absorb heat?

Repeat the experiment once more. This time paint both pans black. Cover one pan with aluminum foil. Leave the other uncovered. In which pan does the water get hotter?

Based on your experiments, what color containers would you use to absorb solar energy? How would you reflect away unwanted sunlight?

FURTHER READING

Books

Adams, Richard, C., and Peter H. Goodwin. *Physics Projects for Young Scientists*. New York: Franklin Watts, Inc., 2000.

Bombaugh, Ruth. *Science Fair Success, Revised and Expanded*. Springfield, N.J.: Enslow Publishers, Inc., 1999.

Dickinson, Terence. *Nightwatch: A Practical Guide to Viewing the Universe*. Third edition. Buffalo, N.Y.: Firefly Books, 1998.

Vogt, Gregory. *Deep Space Astronomy*. Brookfield, Conn.: Twenty-First Century Books, Inc., 1999.

Wroble, Lisa. *Space Science*. Mankato, Minn.: Capstone Press, Inc., 1992.

Internet Addresses

Internet Public Library
<http://www.ipl.org/youth/projectguide>

Nine Planets
<http:/www.seds.org/nineplanets/nineplanets>

StarChild
<http://starchild.gsfc.nasa.gov/docs/StarChild/StarChild.html>

The Ultimate Science Fair Resource
<http://www.scifair.org>

INDEX